CORONET AMONG
THE WEEDS

CORONET AMONG THE WEEDS

Charlotte Bingham

Typeset by Integra Software Services Pvt. Ltd
Printed and bound in Great Britain by CPI Group (UK) Ltd, Croydon

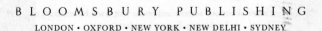

B L O O M S B U R Y   P U B L I S H I N G
LONDON · OXFORD · NEW YORK · NEW DELHI · SYDNEY

BLOOMSBURY PUBLISHING
Bloomsbury Publishing Plc
50 Bedford Square, London, WC1B 3DP, UK

BLOOMSBURY, BLOOMSBURY PUBLISHING and the Diana logo are
trademarks of Bloomsbury Publishing Plc

First published in Great Britain by William Heinemann Ltd, 1963

Copyright © Charlotte Bingham, 1963 and 2019

Charlotte Bingham has asserted her right under the Copyright, Designs and
Patents Act, 1988, to be identified as Author of this work

A catalogue record for this book is available from the British Library

Library of Congress Cataloguing-in-Publication data has been applied for

ISBN: PB: 978-1-5266-0869-7; EBOOK: 978-1-5266-0885-7

8 10 9 7 5 3 1

PREFACE

Dear Reader,

If you have shelled out some of your hard earned on this slim volume from long ago then it might help to know a little about how it came into being and changed the life of its teenage author forever.

I was the daughter of two professional writers. At the tender age of six I was left with my grandmother while my mother went off to something called 'rehearsal'. She had written a comedy which had gone from the Royal Court Theatre to the West End where it had a very successful run. My father on the other hand wrote crime novels. Added to which my aunt was a novelist. So writing and writers were everywhere in my childhood.

But as I discovered, wanting is one thing – breathing life into your words quite another. My first attempt at the age of ten was a crime novel entitled 'Death's Ticket'. My parents were impressed with what they called the 'plot'. I am sorry to tell you I learned to hate that word. Every time one of my family saw me scribbling they would ask 'what's your plot?' or they would say 'I hope you've got a plot'. A famous writer told my aunt you should be able to write a novel about someone going to post a letter. I know what he meant but having attempted it at the age of somewhere around eleven I have to tell you it is no picnic.

Actually writing about a picnic would be a ball compared to that blasted letter. By the age of twelve I was attempting to write romantic literature at which my aunt was very successful, but my pen kept faltering when it came to the hero and heroine kissing. Talk about where do the noses go – I had no idea where anything went.

All in all, by the age of seventeen I had almost given up on the idea of ever being able to string words together and be able to write more than 'by Charlotte Bingham', which I did quite a lot – only trouble being there was nothing preceding it. And still the word 'plot' haunted me, until I started to go to the Opera and read the programme notes. Suddenly the clouds parted – here at last were plots written out clearly and precisely. This gave me hope. I started a novel which was destined to be full of people being very heavy towards the heroine, but then life intervened – not for her, for me — and I became a debutante and went to endless balls dressed in evening dresses and wearing long white gloves. Many of the balls were delightful and very romantic.

But still the stone in my — usually a satin evening shoe — was this feeling that I hadn't completed a book, until one evening when I moaned to my parents that after so many parties and balls I hadn't yet met 'a superman'.

'Write about that,' they said. 'Stop writing dreary, write comedy.' Well, by that time I was causing mayhem at MI5 as a secretary (see *MI5 and Me*) — and had only evenings to write. My social life had taken me to the downstairs bar at the London Ritz where I noted that a tomato juice was only two shillings, and the nuts and crisps were free! This was great as the lunch hour at MI5 was an hour and a half, so down I went to the lower floor with my pen and paper and scribbled my comedy, closely watched by Laurie and Edward the barmen who replenished the nuts at very regular intervals. Of course the Society balls and parties had to go by the wayside. Now there was a centre to my life — I was writing a book to make people laugh. Inevitably I suffered a wobble (page 108). Was it funny? My father, realising this, wrote me a note: 'Carry on kid, you might make a hundred pounds!' That was incentive enough, for, as you will discover in the book – the bank manager rather haunted our house.

Finally the book was finished.

It was April and I was on 'safe lock up' duty at MI5. There was a light spring pink to the sky. As I sauntered down Bond Street towards Piccadilly I conceived of a revolutionary idea. I would go to the downstairs Ritz Bar – even though it was not in my lunch hour. Laurie and Edward did their best to conceal their surprise.

What to drink? A tomato juice seemed a bit tame, so I ordered something I had never drunk before – but which I thought was the kind of drink that a mature writer should down. I was looking at it with some trepidation when a voice at my shoulder said, 'Charlotte Bingham, what are you doing seated at the Ritz Bar with a whisky in front of you?'

It was my father's agent looking as good humoured and relaxed as he always did. Thereafter followed a great deal of banter centred on my having finished my first book, and – to this day I wouldn't know why – he insisted he would like to read it. I actually tried to dissuade him, but a few days later, it being Easter, he retired to his country house and read what was then entitled 'Search for Superman'.

Of course I never dreamed that he would like it. I imagined he might give me a pat on the head and tell me to go on trying. Instead he rang me at MI5 and said 'I can sell this anywhere. I'll be in touch.'

And he was. Another telephone call the following day and he told me he had just had an offer from Heinemann for £350. It didn't seem possible. I stared round the room after I put the receiver down. It seemed to have changed, it was full of colour and light. I had always dreamed of becoming a writer, and now at long, long last, at the what-seemed-to-me-an-already-ancient age of eighteen, was a WRITER. From now on it would be 'Something Something Something' by Charlotte Bingham. I say 'Something Something Something' because Heinemann didn't like the title and I was, rightly, told to change it. And so *Coronet Among the Weeds* came into being.

I thought that was that, and as far as I was concerned that was quite enough to last me for the next eighteen years. But, probably because of my age, *Coronet Among the Weeds* became of immediate interest to the press. When Heinemann flew with it to the legendary Frankfurt Book Fair they gave out chapters on the plane, so that by the time they arrived at the airport all sorts of other publishers were interested, and it sold to ten other foreign publishers (I am still very big in Albania). It was bought by a Sunday newspaper for serialisation. By now my parents were less than happy. They had always thought I might sell it, but not that I would also become improbably famous – and improbably famous I had become. There were vast posters all over the country advertising the serialisation – pictures of their daughter everywhere, and photographers from all over the world besieged the house. Fed up with all the attention I was getting, they banished me to France. In those dim and distant days no one could refuse parental edicts until they were twenty-one.

I reappeared some months later to be guest of honour at a Foyles Literary Luncheon held at the Dorchester with a glittering top table of famous people. I learned that speech so well I was saying it in my sleep, nevertheless I went so white before the hammer went down and the words 'LORDS LADIES AND GENTLEMEN, pray silence for Miss Charlotte Bingham' – that the press table who had noted my extreme pallor sent me a note: 'cheer up, it will be over soon!'

I remember the end of the speech in which I wished that we lived in a world 'where manuscripts were never sent back and flowers would grow under our feet.' At any rate Heinemann were terribly pleased and Christina Foyle told them she had never heard cheers like it – which I put down to deep sympathy for my extreme youth.

After that my life became almost too incredible – with author tours and television shows and a stay at the Plaza in New York which was so extended that the staff nicknamed me 'the second Eloise'. I was the toast of the Harvard Pudding Club, and met many famous writers who were kind beyond words.

I still hardly believe what happened to me, but it did, and there is no denying the fact that it was a wonderful start to what turned into a life of writing. However before you read on dear reader, remember that this was written a long, long time ago, by an eighteen-year-old in an attic bedroom on a borrowed typewriter. I only hope it raises a smile.

I

I was thinking in bed the other night I must have been out with nearly three hundred men, and I still haven't found a superman. I don't know what a superman is. But I know there must be one somewhere. So does Migo. Migo's my girlfriend, she's a good thing. She's not soppy, but she agrees with me that somewhere there must be a superman. Actually I think most girls believe in a superman. I mean they don't really believe all that phoney stuff you hear them jazzing on about. You know, like girls who look you dead pan in the face drawing nervously on a cigarette and come out with that corny line about men only wanting 'one thing'. That's when they're about seventeen and when you meet them a couple of years later they're still dragging nervously at their cigarettes, but carrying on about their careers.

Then you get the ones who go on about parties, and spend the whole time asking you if you know people or if you're going somewhere for the weekend. It's like parties are a sort of nervous habit with them. And the way they go on about knowing people. You can't know everyone. They're like that nutty saint who wanted to empty the sea into his sandpit. No, hell. I've got it wrong. It was this angel who was scooping up the sea and emptying it into his sandpit, and this saint told him, 'You'll never do it, boy.' Someone ought to tell them. Anyway, both these types of girls anyone with half an eye can see are just waiting around for a superman; and they don't even let themselves know, but they are.

Actually I think what a Frenchman once said to me is true. He said all little girls were born women because they know how to cham. I think he must have had something. He was rather old but still most girls don't get around to really thinking about a superman till they're about thirteen.

I started playing the 'other woman' role when I was thirteen. We had a Swedish maid. Honestly you wouldn't have known she was Swedish, she was like a huge Spanish woman or something. With black hair and a huge bronzed body, and she had this boy-friend called Mess. Yes, honestly he was called Mess. He said it was short for a Persian name. He was Persian. Anyway, he spoke English with an American accent and wore denim jeans, and my grandmother set the dogs on him every time she saw him hanging round our gate. She doesn't like foreigners. Actually she doesn't like many people. She's always going on about 'all those filthy disgusting people', and it's no good telling her she's one of them because she won't believe you.

Anyway, this Mess, our Swede was mad about him. She used to lie around on our lawn in a *broderie anglaise* bikini hoping he'd get by the dogs and my grandmother. My mother used to make her take me to Brighton for the day, and Mess used to meet us off the train and we'd go and have coffee with him. I used to have an awful time keeping him from seeing my profile. I had a complex about not having a chin. It was maddening, because this Swede had one. And I used to get a stiff neck trying not to turn my head, but anyway it was quite fun. And then I read if you tied a scarf under your chin at night it helped, and honestly I think it made a difference because it's not too bad now. Also I used to tie my hands on to the rail above my head so all the blood drained from them and they looked dead-white and aristocratic. It was quite a business getting into bed.

Anyway Mess used to walk to the bus-stop with us, and then he and this Swede would start kissing.

Honestly, you've never seen anything like it. I timed them once, two and a half minutes for one kiss. I don't know if that's a record, but it's not bad. She must have had good lungs that girl.

Then Mess started going to London during the week and just coming back for weekends, and sometimes our Swede couldn't get the weekend off so she used to send me to see him with letters. I don't think she was very intelligent. He had a room in a house down the road, and we used to play his gramophone, and he'd say I had pretty hair, but I still had hell keeping him from seeing my profile.

The thing is, I didn't particularly think he was attractive, but I wanted to see if I could win him from that Swede and her chin. Only for fun, to sort of see if I could do it. It wasn't malicious or anything. So, anyhow, she used to go and see him in London sometimes during the week, and she always asked me what she should wear and how she should do her hair and everything. So one day I got a bit bored and I told her she looked wonderful with her hair all flat, and wearing this thick black dress. So she went to London like that. Honestly, I don't think she could have been very intelligent. 'Course Mess told her she looked awful, and sent her back by the next train. Actually it wasn't much fun after that because the Swede went back to Sweden, and the whole thing lost its point, but anyway it was quite interesting.

After the Swede went back to Sweden, we moved back to London. No, just before we moved back to London I went to my first dance. It was hell, honestly. No one wanted to dance with me because I was thirteen and they were all fifteen, and they kept on doing these Scottish reels and everything. And my parents were there, and my father kept winking at me as if it didn't matter, but it did, so I went into the kitchen and talked to the dogs. At least they didn't have spots like half those damn boys. It's a funny thing about dogs when you're young. You feel much more for your dog than most of your relations. Except your grandfather or something. I know more girls who start crying about their dogs and their grandfathers than anything else.

Anyway after that dance I swore I'd go back to that place when I was fifteen and make everyone mad to dance with me. Funny thing actually because I did.

When we moved back to London we stopped having maids because the house was too small, and I spent most of the time at the movies with my cousin. I was fat and she had spots so we had plenty to talk about. Then my mother said I should go to dancing classes. They were hell too, no kidding. All these boys looking at you, and this man banging away on the piano and this woman pushing you in and out of eightsomes and things. Then you had to pretend to be things. Or run up and down pretending you'd got a nightie on. Honestly, try running up and down pretending you've got a nightie on with a whole lot of boys of fifteen sneering at you. And they had such awful faces. And they were either terribly tall or absolutely tiny. So you spent the whole time walking backwards talking to the bottom button on a jacket, or the top of a small greasy head. Honestly, it was murder.

Then a girl at school's mother started getting up this Charity Dance. And everyone decided to go, and my mother said she'd give a buffet supper beforehand. I didn't know any boys, so my mother asked a friend of her's son, and my cousin asked a boy she knew when she was four. I didn't have a dress so we had one made at the dressmaker and my mother bought me some flowers to pin on my shoulder, and I was a bit thinner. When they all arrived the boys turned out to be rather a good thing. Even my cousin's friend whom she hadn't seen since she was four. Rather a lucky strike really.

Then what the hell do you think happened? This girl's boyfriend got measles. Least he rang up and said he had measles, and she just turned up without anybody. Honestly, it was absolutely typical. Just because she was two years older than all of us and madly swoony she knew she was okay, thank you. If anyone was going to sit out it wasn't going to be her. She wasn't even the sort of girl you could like much. She went round madly pretending she wasn't swoony, but still, a terrible lot of people thought she was awfully nice. Especially men.

Anyhow I did all right at the dance until the eightsome started up, and suddenly everyone had partners except me. And that girl was looking coy with my partner. So I had to go and sit behind a pillar on one of those ghastly gilt chairs. And when it stopped and I started to jump up and rush back to claim a partner, some fiendish voice shouted encore and it started all over again. I swear it was that girl. Honestly, there was nothing she wouldn't stop at, really there wasn't, she even came up and apologised afterwards. And she used to take all these girls around with her to parties and introduce them to boys and say how clever they were to these boys, and of course these boys would never look at them again; they'd just swoon round her saying they were terribly glad she wasn't clever.

Except for that damn eightsome, the dance was quite fun. Afterwards we all arranged to go to a movie the next day. This boy who was my partner stayed the night with us because he lived in Surrey. He ate up all the trifles from the night before for breakfast. My mother was awfully pleased, and she thought he had nice manners. I liked him too but he didn't make me swoon. You know. It was this other girl's partner I liked. We all did actually. He had one of those boy-next-door faces. He was there when we went to the movies, but this girl sat next to him until the elastic in her knickers went and she had to go to the loo and find a safety-pin. Then I moved up and sat next to him. We were both laughing because it was quite funny, and he said, 'Are you going to the rugger match tomorrow?' and I said, 'No.'

I didn't see him again after that until the Easter holidays when me and this girl got asked to a dance by the daughter of a friend of my mother. We had to take our own partners, so she brought this boy-next-door type and I didn't know anyone I wanted to bring so I didn't take anyone.

The dance was in a sort of hall, and there was a band and a friend of my mother's played the drums. He was damned good actually. Anyway, I didn't have a partner so I had to dance with this boy called George. Honestly, it was terrible. He had glasses and his hair came up to my chin; he was much worse than anything I'd met at the dancing classes. And he just couldn't dance. I mean, he couldn't even do a straight walk in time to the music, and we had to do this shuffle up and down *because* he couldn't manage the corners. And this other girl was having a fabulous time with her old boy-next-door type, whirling by because he danced absolutely marvellously, and they kept on smiling at me so I had to pretend George was my dream come true.

Then the other girl was asked to dance by someone else and the boy-next-door type came up and asked me to dance. We danced a waltz and then the lights went out and he whirled me about in the candlelight and he kissed my cheek just before the lights went up. I nearly died it was so romantic. Then George came up and asked me for my address and I gave it to him just to show the boy-next-door type he wasn't the only thing around.

Do you know that stupid ass wrote to me. I didn't get many letters, so of course my mother wanted to know who had written to me. I just said it was from a girl. You wouldn't believe it, but he wrote to me at school too. All about him playing squash. It made me sick to think of him playing squash, bouncing up and down and sweating. My cousin laughed her head off though; she said I should keep the letter, but I just couldn't bear to. It made me sick.

I forgot about the corny old boy-next-door type after two different girls told me they were swooning about him in the cloakroom. I hate obvious men. When girls go on about a man being attractive he never is. He's just stomping round *being* madly attractive. You know, 'Here's super old me. Now swoon everyone.' Of course some girls find everyone attractive. No, honestly, they really do. It's not the anything-in-trousers technique, they really think all these types are swoony. My mother says her sister's like that. She says she tells my mother she's got the most super young man coming to dinner and a bottle-nosed man of forty comes in. Rather sad really.

After that the most awful thing happened. I got this nervous reaction about this uncle of mine. Least he's not a real uncle, he's an uncle by marriage. He's frightfully nice actually. But God it was boring having this nervous reaction. I wasn't in love with him or anything, I just went this awful colour every time he came into the room or said something. A friend of mine had the same thing, only she went this colour every time anyone at all looked at her. So we used to do this thing. Every time we felt a blush coming on we'd look at something white. It really helped, honestly, it was fantastic. I still do it sometimes, even now.

Well, me and this girl kept on having bets about things. You know:

'Bet you I get a bra before you do.'

'Bet you I'm engaged before you are.'

And so on. Anyway she'd won on the bra stakes. She had a bigger bust than me. So I was absolutely determined to be kissed before she was. Only it's not so damned easy, because you've got to get someone to kiss you. It didn't count if you went up and kissed them. Well, we were all at this curry party a girl-friend gave in her flat. And we sat around on the floor eating curry and wearing jeans and shirts and things. Then everyone started sort of dancing a bit, and this boy in a kilt did a Highland-fling in the hall.

But I just went on dancing with this same boy all the time, because I knew if you wanted someone to kiss you, you had to dance with him the whole evening. I didn't like dancing with just one person, but I wanted to win this bet. I'd got quite good at talking to people by then. I mean I didn't feel shy or anything, and I think he rather liked me. I quite liked him actually, and he didn't have spots or anything. I did draw the line at being kissed the first time by someone with spots. I mean you can take betting too far.

Anyway, they switched the corny old light off for the last dance, and he said,

'Can I kiss you?'

And I said,

'All right.'

So he did.

I was jolly disappointed. I don't know what I expected to happen, but it was so dull. Honestly, I remember thinking what a lot of fuss people made about nothing. He kissed me again by the back door after he'd driven me home. I thought I'd better let him, though I didn't like it much, but anyway I won that bet.

Then this boy called Mervyn whom I'd met at the dancing classes rang me up and asked me to this party. He just said it was a party so I put on a sort of party dress and flowers in my hair, and me and a girlfriend went to his flat. She was wearing a party dress too. When we arrived at his flat we rang the bell but nothing happened, so I pushed the door and it opened. So I said,

'Let's go in.'

It was one of those flats with long expensive corridors. You know. You wouldn't know you were walking the carpets are so thick. The only way you can tell is that your legs keep moving. Anyway we walked along these corridors, and kept peering in and out of different rooms, but they were all just terribly quiet and expensive. Then we got to the end of this corridor and we heard a gramophone going, so we went in. And it was terribly dark, nothing but a few candles. I was a bit scared and I said,

'Shall we go?'

But this other girl said,

'No, hell let's stay and see what happens.'

I couldn't help thinking about my mother. She gets a bit conventional sometimes. I didn't think it was her sort of party. But we found Mervyn, and he was a bit drunk, but he introduced us to these other friends of his who were quite nice, and we all danced a bit, and I didn't feel so nervous. And there was a boy sitting in a corner reading a book and laughing, and they all asked if I'd read it. I hadn't. So they said I should: it was a frightfully rude book someone had bought in

Paris. But I said I didn't want to. Honestly, I'm not a prude, but I hate that awful commercial-traveller attitude. You know: it *must* be funny because it's rude. Actually I think the English are rather awful like that. Anyway, this boy called Mervyn kept on giving me these drinks that tasted just like lemonade, but I realised they couldn't be when I started feeling dizzy. I said to the boy I was dancing with,

'I feel a bit drunk.'

And he said,

'You look a bit drunk.'

So I went and looked in the mirror, and I looked awful. The flowers were hanging off their kirby grip, and someone had spilt something on my dress. I said to this boy,

'Maybe I'll feel better when I've had something to eat.'

But he said why didn't I try walking in a straight line and that he'd help me. I just couldn't do it. So they got this other boy and they all helped me along very slowly, but I looked so funny that we kept on giggling. All the time, though, I kept on wondering what my mother would say if she saw me. It was some thought. Honestly, she'd have had a fit. Then Mervyn started throwing glasses at the wall. I think he must have felt insecure or something. He just kept on picking up these glasses and throwing them at the wall. There was nothing wrong with the glasses, he just kept on breaking them. Mind you, his parents were divorced.

I went up to him, and he stopped throwing glasses, and I said I wanted to go home and thank you for the lovely party. But he said I couldn't possibly go home, I must come to this night club he knew. I said I didn't like night clubs. Actually I'd never been in one. He said I would adore this one, so everyone got into a taxi, and I had to go too because I didn't have the taxi money to take me home. When we arrived, there wasn't enough money for everyone to go in, but I wasn't going to miss seeing inside now I was there, so six of us went in with Mervyn. It was as corny as anything inside. Honestly, all that money, and there wasn't any decent vice anywhere. It was just rather dark and there was this old band playing away, and a lot of old men sitting around with women and thinking and eating. And a few of them were creeping up and down the floor with these stupid-looking blondes. And that was all. Still it made something to talk about at school.

Then Migo and I decided to give a party. We made up a rhyming invitation, sitting on the radiator at school, and she typed it out on cards with one of the nuns' typewriters. They looked rather good and we knew a lot of people by then, what with the dancing classes and things. My mother said we could have the party in our house. She spent days putting nuts on trifles and cheese in celery and things, and we put the food in the dining-room downstairs and kept the drawing-room for dancing and asked this woman in to wash up. All the parents went off for the evening as soon as they saw everyone arriving. We had this huge bowl of punch in the drawing-room and rock-and-roll records.

Actually it was quite gay. Everyone started dancing and playing these games where you have to stand on a matchbox with a name written on your back and try and find someone to match the name on your back. Then whoever finds the person that matches them, without getting off the matchbox, wins. I went down to the kitchen when they started passing grapefruits under their chins. There was this woman there washing up.

'The floor's going to give in,' she said.

I looked at the ceiling, and it did look a bit bendy.

'It oughtn't to be allowed,' she said.

She wasn't very nice. And she had this nervous tic. She kept on licking her finger and pushing at her forehead with it. Like one of those fly-catching frogs with long tongues.

I went upstairs with more glasses, and they'd all started dancing in our garden. It's not very big, but anyway they did. And, do you know, it was fantastic the next morning. There wasn't a single thing growing there. It gave my father a bit of a shock I can tell you. Honestly, one moment he was looking for greenfly and the next he was just standing around with all this earth.

'Your father's very hurt,' my mother said.

It's always much worse if they're hurt. I think she knows that.

'A friend of mine broke the punch-bowl,' I said.

'Are you sure he's a friend?' she said. She can be rather sarcastic sometimes. The drawing-room smelt like a pub for weeks, but I think everyone enjoyed themselves.

Well, the thing was what with one thing and another I was nearly sixteen by this time. So my mother said I should leave school. She doesn't believe in girls knowing a frightful lot or going to university. She says they're mucky, the rooms of girls who go to university, I mean. She just thinks girls should have a bit of culture, and know how to cook and keep things clean. Actually I don't know if she isn't right sometimes. I mean all those suffragettes and things, no one gets up for you on the Tube now. I think it must have been quite fun when women were rather mysterious, and men didn't know all about them. Look at the end-product of women being free. I mean, go on, look at it. It's a poor old career girl sitting in her digs wondering whether she ought to ring up her boy-friend or not. It makes you think sometimes.

Anyway, my mother said she thought I ought to leave school. The nuns didn't want me to, but she did. So I did. I was jolly sad to leave school actually. I went to the most super convent. All the nuns were marvellous; honestly, they were the most broadminded people you've ever met. I get very cross about nuns. People always go on and on about them not knowing anything and shutting themselves away from life and all that stuff. Like the saints. I bet if you met a saint he'd make Wyatt Earp look like a weed. Really, they had to be frightfully tough.

Migo went to a convent too. She left when she was sixteen with me. She wanted to go to Paris. We both did. We used to sit about and talk about it, and make up the most marvellous things that were going to happen to us. But this nun asked Migo if she thought she had a vocation. Honestly, she really thought Migo would make a good nun. We couldn't get over it. I remember I was so stunned I kept on asking her if it was true. I ask you – Migo a nun. They never asked me if I wanted to be a nun. I don't think I ever showed any tendencies actually. Most girls do. I remember I once asked my mother what she'd do if I became a nun, and she said I couldn't possibly, it was too expensive. She's quite holy, but you have to give them this lump sum when you go in, and we never seem to have lump sums.

Actually I don't think that nun could have known Migo very well. Anyone can see she's just looking for a superman.

2

Just before I went to Paris with Migo, I fell in love. It was the older man routine. Though he wasn't that old actually, but he was a grown-up and I wasn't. I didn't like it much, being in love I mean. But I was quite resigned. It's just one of those things you have to go through, like teething or something. I fell in love with him for a funny reason. It sounds stupid. But he didn't flirt with me or anything. And he had the most innocent eyes. I know it sounds soppy for a man, but they were really innocent. 'Course he was amusing and good looking too, but that was the main reason, this sort of innocence I mean.

He was an actor, and he was staying with us till he got a flat. He used to rehearse in his room, and I would sit on the stairs for hours listening to him. That's the thing about being in love, you find yourself doing nutty things, and you don't even think they're nutty. I knew a girl once who was madly in love with a married man, and she used to stand outside his house with her mother's hats on, waiting for his wife to go out. She didn't want the wife to know what she looked like. I said, didn't it get a bit boring, and she said, yes, but it was worth it.

It's pretty funny living in the same house as someone you're in love with. I used to have breakfast and everything with this actor, and sit on the kitchen stairs and talk. And he used to lend me his aftershave lotion to stop my mother smelling when my dogs made pools on the carpet.

Migo and I had to go by train to Paris because of my luggage. My mother's got funny ideas about luggage. I once watched her packing for a weekend. She kept walking round her room muttering and putting clothes in suitcases.

'I must take my gold lamé for drinks, and my blue for dinner, and six jumpers because the heating's so bad, and my tweed in case we beagle.'

'You don't know how to beagle,' I said. But she said you never knew.

Even when I'd gone to Paris she never stopped sending me parcels with more clothes and medicines in them. She made me swear on the family Bible, that my aunt's poodle chewed up, that I wouldn't buy French medicines and to send her a telegram if I was ill. When I was ill, they never gave me anything but suppositories. Honestly, whatever you had wrong with you they just said:

'*Ah-ha, il faut les suppositoires.*'

Nothing much happened on the journey to Paris except someone was sick down my coat. I told my mother when I rang her after we arrived, but she wasn't interested. She was annoyed about this person not waiting till they got to the loo. She said there was no excuse, you could always feel it coming on, and really it was too annoying all down my nice new coat.

I was staying with a Marquis in Paris. A very nice Marquis actually, with six children and a very old flat near the Pont des Arts. They were de-moneyed aristocrats, like my family. Only I think we enjoy it more than they did. I think you either do or you don't. I know my mother's jolly relieved; she says she couldn't have stood all those draughty castles. But some people miss them – their castles I mean – they sit about and regret them and talk about their ancestors. Ancestors are hell's boring. I've had to sit through evening-fuls of them. It's all right if there are lots of people, because they all talk quite happily about their own, and no one listens. Like when everyone starts talking about their fillings. They all have their fingers in their mouths pointing out their fillings so no one listens to anyone else, but they're quite happy. But, if you get only a couple of people telling you about the Battle of Bilsworth Common, you've got to listen. Then sure as hell they'll suddenly find they're related and go all the way back to the Black Death, and you've had it.

Migo was staying with a family of Communists. She said they weren't at all bad, they just kept on going on about Moscow. Everything in Moscow was marvellous, rather like the Irish and the Old Country. Migo got a bit bored of Moscow at every meal, so she said, why didn't they go and live there if it was so marvellous. They said, no, they weren't rats to desert a sinking ship, they preferred to fight for Communism in Paris. What I said to Migo was, I bet they'd get browned off if all the women in Paris looked like the women in Moscow. I bet they would too.

Migo said that except for Moscow they were quite nice. Amusing too, which is unusual for Communists really. On the whole they're a bit inclined to be po-faced. When I was about fourteen I got a bit atheistic, so I thought I'd have a go at being a Communist. My mother was frightful squashing. She said I'd never be any good, I was far too happy and washed too much. And I hadn't got a grudge. Apparently it's no good unless you've got a grudge.

A friend of Migo's told us about these lectures for foreigners at the Sorbonne, so we went along and enrolled. I don't know if you know what the Sorbonne looks like inside, but they have this enormous room like the Roman Forum with tiers of seats, and the lecturer stands in the middle on a dais. We were fascinated by all the types that went to these lectures. Absolutely every nationality you can think of. The Americans took down screeds of notes, but the Chinese students never had a piece of paper on them, they just seemed to have brains like tape-recorders that sucked everything in. One Chinese boy I used to sit next to, would just gracefully close his eyes when the lecture started and sit immobile till it ended, then he would open them and look inscrutable.

The first week we were there, a man stood on his head during one of the lectures. Everyone began to laugh, because being in a lecture is rather like being in church; anything seems funny. I asked Migo what he was doing, and she said he was either a Yogi or a beatnik. I was awfully pleased I hadn't missed him, because he was the first one I'd ever seen. I'd led a bit of a sheltered life, what with one thing and another.

I got to know the French quite well living with this French family. They're different from the English.

They cook, talk a lot, and don't wash much. They're more intelligent than the English because they never stop taking exams. They start when they're five, then just never stop. And they spend the whole time asking each other about them: when they're going to take them, how they're going to do them, whether they passed, why they failed, when the next one is. It's a sort of social game really. The French have a lot of social games. And they have all these rules about what you can say *dans le salon* and what you can't say *dans le salon*. You don't have to be *dans le salon* not to be able to say these things you're not meant to, you can be anywhere. But you just can't say them. There's not much you can say actually, except how's aunt Ag and the weather and stuff. Migo didn't have trouble with *le salon* because of being with Communists. *Le salon* is absolutely not on with Communists.

I never had a bath the whole time I was in Paris. The thing was they had a bath but, if you turned on the taps, the ceiling fell down, so there wasn't much point. I didn't mind not having a bath, but I got a guilt complex about not washing. I spent the whole time thinking I was dirty and standing in a bucket of water. It was stupid, because not many people wash when they have a bath. I know my father doesn't. He just thinks and has a bit of a rest. Though not if my mother can help it. As soon as she knows he's in there she remembers that she's left half her things behind, or she wants to tell him something frightfully important. Then she starts knocking on the door and shouting, but he turns on the taps and pretends he can't hear. Don't blame him really.

I had quite a hard time learning French, because I'm not intelligent. It's funny because everyone else in my family is. But they always say your children take after someone obscure. It makes me a bit nervous when I look at some of my relations. My mother kept on hoping I'd be intelligent but I was a disappointment. The first school I went to they had this old Montessori method, where you only do what you want to do. It didn't work on me because of not being intelligent. I just had this idea it was more fun to play than to work, and didn't learn to read till I was six.

As soon as I did speak a little French, I started to go to French dances, but I didn't have much success with Frenchmen as long as they knew I was English. They weren't very keen on English girls. Luckily I don't look very English, because I had one grandfather who was French, so they often got let in for something they hadn't bargained for. But they couldn't stand it for

long. So I wrote myself a French dance-type conversation, timed it to last half an hour and learned it off
by heart. It turned out to be a jolly good thing. I'd just
dance away quite happily having this conversation then
I'd change partners and I'd start all over again. They
all said what a marvellous accent I had and that you'd
never think I was English, and I'd tell them about this
French grandfather of mine, and they'd say – ah – that
explained everything. They even thought I was witty.

One thing about French men though. They can
dance. Which is more than Englishmen can. Englishmen
scoop you up if you're small like me and press you
against the side of their ear, and leave you there for
the rest of the evening. I once saw a girl scooped
right out of her dress, only this nit who'd scooped her
was holding her so tight that neither of them could see
what had happened.

There was a Count I danced a lot with in Paris, and
he used to take me to the movies, and teach me French
argot. French *argot* is much more fun than *le salon*
French. I got a bit muddled sometimes, and I told a
Duchess that I thought French tarts were excellent. It
was a bit embarrassing I can tell you. Actually French
tarts look jollier than English ones. I had a friend who
lived next door to a few. She said they were always

27

singing and laughing and things. Except for one who was called Jeannette la Noire. She was always dressed in black and had long dyed black hair and she never smiled, just played the violin. Of course my mother says that tarts with a heart of gold are a myth. But my grandfather used to say that some of the nicest people he knew were tarts. What my grandmother wanted to know was how he knew. But my mother says that it was different in his day, and you don't get such a good class of girl nowadays. Of course peak tart-time was the Regency days, there's no doubt about that. They had a much better time than the wives, and influence over the old Iron Duke and people.

Migo didn't go to many dances, because her Communists didn't have much social life. She said they used to have men in mackintoshes coming to see them at midnight, but none of them seemed to give dances. So she joined a students' society which gave parties in a cellar, and stately home visits once a fortnight on Thursdays. The cellar parties could be quite fun because a lot of Sorbonne people went, and they had a jazz band. The Marquis's wife didn't approve of students or cellars, so I just used to tell her I was doing a cultural course on Eastern philosophy. There were a lot of quite cultured Arabs about so I didn't think it was much of a lie. A friend of mine called Daphne fell in love with one of them. She wanted to marry him and go back to Arabia with him and everything. I thought it was a good idea. My favourite saint tried to convert the Arabs. He only ever converted one, and he went back to being a Mohammedan as soon as this old saint was dead. That's why he was my favourite saint. Also, he lived it up like anything before he started being a saint.

Daphne didn't marry her Arab in the end actually. She said he wasn't genuine enough. He didn't have a camel or wear robes or live in a tent or anything. The Arab was furious when she stopped going out with him. He went round telling everyone it was because he was an Arab and she was prejudiced. It wasn't that at all; she just stopped being in love with him. But he wouldn't believe her.

Some of the cellar parties could get a bit wild. Beatniks got too hep and started throwing things. Sometimes it wasn't too dangerous, but if they really went potty all the girls had to lock themselves in the loos till they calmed down a bit. It was rather boring sitting in the loos but it was better than nothing. We made up stories and shouted them over the top at each other, because you can't play hopscotch or anything much in a loo, it's too small. Occasionally I climbed over the top and had a look at one of the others, but mostly we just told these stories till everyone had quietened down a bit. Once I climbed over to see a girl and she started crying.

'It's all right, this always happens, they soon stop,' I said.

But she kept on crying and saying,

'I'm *au pair!*'

'We'll think up a super excuse, don't worry,' I said.

Then she just kept on saying it was all right for me but she was *au pair,* so in the end I got back into my own loo again. There wasn't much I could do.

I thought she was a bit soppy crying, but you had to feel sorry for her. Honestly being *au pair* in France is *pas un joke.* It sounds all right, that's the trouble. What usually happens is you get this poor girl who wants to learn French, but doesn't want to go to finishing-school. So all her relations and friends write off to people they know, and eventually someone comes up with a frightfully posh family who have millions of servants and just want someone to speak a few words of English to one of their nine children for two hours every morning. Of course this poor creature arrives with dreams of gallant Frenchmen paying her court, only to find that she's washing up till midnight, and the only Frenchman around is old Monsieur wheezing away at supper every night. One of Migo's cousins went *au pair* to look after a girl of fifteen. She had to speak English to this drip in the morning, walk her in the afternoons, and get this – give her a bath at night. Honestly, she was really meant to bath this huge great girl every night, wash behind her ears for her and everything. She went on strike after a bit, she really couldn't stand it. She said the girl's feet were so big.

Except for the old Count and a few French types I met at dances, I didn't have many boyfriends. Migo and I mostly went around with a mixed bunch of people. There were some English cads, and a lot of pre-deb type girls who went around behaving badly with various weeds. They really were weeds these boys, anyone could see they were. I couldn't understand these girls swooning over them; I don't think they were in love with them. They were just bored. Nothing to do so they let these weeds drool over them. I can't understand people going on like that. I mean, okay super if you're in love with somebody, but just any old drip because you've got nothing better to do – I don't get it, honestly I don't. I mean you should have *seen* some of them. Not even the cat would have brought them in. And they used to do it all over the place. You couldn't even go to the movies, and you'd look down the row after five minutes and everyone was locked in some-one else's arms. Anyway, Migo said it was unhygienic.

There was this girl called Jennifer like that. She was really embarrassing with these complete weeds.

'Do you like them making love to you?' I asked her once.

She gave me a deep look, then said, 'No.'

'Well, why do you let them?' I said.

'If you'd had a father like mine, you'd know why,' she said.

'What did he do to you?'

'He gave me an inferiority complex.'

'What's that got to do with weeds making love to you?'

'I don't feel so inferior,' she said.

One or two girls went Latin Quarter all in cap-ital letters. They weren't very good at it, but anyway they did. You know: grew their hair, dyed it and didn't wash. It would have been all right if they'd been amusing, but they weren't. They just slept with a few beards and went round talking about it rather loudly, pretty boring really. I mean it's not as if it's difficult.

I suppose youthful impressions of Paris are corny. Actually I suppose Paris is rather corny. I didn't think so. Even accidents were fun. Everyone shouted happily, the whole boulevard stopped and took sides, then they all went home to lunch and discussed it over the pâté. There was one thing that was a bore though, and that was being hooted by men. It's not a compliment, because they just stop and shout at anything when they're not in a hurry. Most of the time Migo and I didn't really mind, we'd just hum a little tune and pretend it wasn't happening. But every now and then we'd get dead tired of it, so I'd shut one eye and limp, and Migo would help me along looking very po. It always worked. They wouldn't whistle or anything, just pass us by looking rather sad.

We went round one or two of the old monuments, and the Louvre and all that. It was okay if I went with Migo or somebody, but every now and then the Marquis's wife would arrange for one of the daughters to go with me, and that was hell. They were a bit serious about culture, 'specially the Egyptians, and there were all these mummies in the Louvre. Genuine ones all right, but they all looked the same to me, so I'd take a few peppermints in with me and sit on a mummy till it was time to go home.

I liked the art galleries though. I've always wanted to draw, but I've never been any good. At school I had a cart-horse fixation. I never stopped drawing these nine-legged cart-horses everywhere, I don't know why. Anyway, my favourite art gallery was the one with all the Impressionists in it. I liked Toulouse-Lautrec one of the best. He was fantastic that man, he really was. He could draw all these things like prostitutes waiting for a medical, and lesbians in bed, but he never made you feel sick. You just thought they were sad and funny and everything. It meant quite a lot to me being able to look at those pictures actually; because, though I thought knew about lesbians and people, I didn't really.

There was one picture of a woman that made me cry. Mind you, anything made me cry then. Honestly, I couldn't even see a beggar in the Metro and I'd start crying all over the place. Anyway, this picture made me cry because this woman had sad feet, they really were the saddest feet you've ever seen, with shoes with droopy rosettes on them. Whenever I was bored I'd go and sit in front of these feet and cry, and when the actor I was in love with came to Paris for a few days I was dying to show him. I kept on going on about this picture, and eventually he got to see it.

Do you know, he didn't like it. It nearly killed me, don't ask me why, but it did. I mean it didn't matter that he didn't like it, he was nice enough without having to like this picture too, but I still went on minding about him not liking it. I told someone about it afterwards, and they said it was one of the facts of life. You just can't share everything with your superman. You have to tell yourself they're super, and forget the rest.

It was jolly nice when that actor came to Paris actually. We didn't do much, just walked around and looked at everything. We didn't talk much either, come to think of it, or make love or anything. It doesn't sound very exciting, but it was. I cried when he went. That's the trouble when you do meet a superman.

Paris is the best place to be if you've got to be hope-lessly in love, because of its being so gay, as I was just saying. And Migo shut me up if I started going on too much. You can be hell's boring when you're in love. I mean you try to think it's all a big joke but you just can't. You try and think of things to make you laugh but you just don't find them funny. In fact I don't think love on the whole is very jokey really.

Then old François caused a diversion. Poor old François. He was the most good-looking man you've ever seen. You know, tall, slim, bronzed, Grecian features and a medal on a piece of leather round his neck. He played the guitar in a relaxed way, giving you deep looks every now and then. I never know what to do when people give me deep looks. I usually stare out of the window and pretend I'm thinking.

I met him because I wore a hat for a bet. You wouldn't think that was very daring unless you've lived round the Left Bank. It's just one of those things you never do, wear a hat. Anyway, I was dared to wear this hat in one of the students' restaurants. Boy, you try it. They drum their knives and forks on the tables until you take it off, shouting *'Chapeau'* like the revolutionaries shouting *'à la guillotine'*. When they all started shouting at me I pretended I didn't understand (it was a very English hat). So old François came up and explained to me in English that I had to take it off, or they'd do it for me. I refused because it was part of the bet that you had to keep it on for ten minutes. I must say I got pretty nervous when they all started to get up and move in on me. I could see my entrails scattered all over the Boul' Mich, and headlines: 'English Student torn to Bits'; 'Peer's Daughter Savaged in Restaurant'. Or only a very small paragraph at the bottom of page six: 'The arm of a woman, believed to be English, was found outside a *pissoir* in Paris last night. The French police are making inquiries.'

I didn't get savaged because old François marched me out of the restaurant, fighting off pursuers. He looked madly noble, guitar in one hand, me in the other. After that I was rather stuck with him. You can't just drop a man who has rescued you from the jaws of death, but he was so damned boring sometimes I wished I'd never won that bet. He thought he was the complete James Dean. Especially on Saturday nights; he'd get terribly droopy over his guitar and look tortured by Life, and all wrought up inside. Then on Sunday he'd be the old Frenchman sitting in church with his mother and wearing one of those ghastly French suits.

Migo and I decided to go home for Christmas, because Christmas abroad can be pretty depressing. I mean they don't do the same thing or anything, and it could make you miserable no one doing the right things. I don't want to be corny, but that's one thing I don't like about being grown-up: Christmas isn't the same. I mean it's funny and all that, and you get presents and stuff, but it's not mysterious like when you were young. Everyone spends the whole time quarrelling. Honestly, our family have all their quarrels at Christmas. They save them up the whole year and then have them at Christmas. They sit about after they've eaten lunch and opened their presents (swopping the bills so they can take them back again) and quarrel about who was rude to whom before the war. You should hear them. I don't know how they remember so far back, but they do.

We went back by boat, because my mother is scared stiff of aeroplanes. I'm not, I like aeroplanes, but my mother doesn't and she was paying so we went by boat. We had tea with a whole lot of finishing-school types on the boat. They were coming home for Christmas too, and a lot of them weren't going back. None of them had learned any French, they hadn't gone to Paris to learn French, just to get finished. I don't know how you get finished but anyway they had. Migo said it was just so that their mothers could stomp about showing off about them.

My mother was waiting on the platform when we got to Victoria. I ran up and kissed her. She held me *away* from her, a look of horror on her face.

'Darling,' she said, 'I wouldn't have recognised you, you're so fat.'

I looked down.

'Gawd, so I am,' I said.

I was too.

3

My cousin said that being fat wasn't so bad as having spots but I didn't believe her. My mother said that she'd got fat when she'd lived in France, and my aunt told me to go and buy a girdle. I drew some money from my savings and went along to a shop in Knightsbridge. A woman with a face like a chamber-pot showed me into a cubicle.

'Madam's measurements?'

I told her, but she didn't believe me. You could see that. She came back with a tape-measure. I took off my coat, and she put the tape-measure round me. She gave little low whistles as she moved down my figure, and they weren't admiration, I can tell you.

'I think Madam has altered a little since she was last measured,' she said, giving me a sarky little smile. Then she came back with a great bundle of these corset things. They were horrible. Monsters with millions of straps and suspenders everywhere. She went out and I put one on. It took some doing, I can tell you, because they had lacing everywhere. Then I looked at myself in the mirror. It was horrible. The suspenders swung round my ankles, and yards of pink caging reached down to my knees. I turned sideways; I felt like suicide. I just thought I'd spend the rest of my life getting into pink cages. I would have jumped out of the window except that woman would have been so thrilled.

The awful thing about being fat is you can't get away from it. Everywhere you go, there it is, all round you: hanging and swinging, yards and yards of it under your arms, everywhere. And everyone else is so thin. When I got out of that shop, *everyone* in Knightsbridge was thin. You've never seen so many thin people. Everyone on the bus was thin, and the girl I went to tea with looked as if she'd had mange. She tried on my belt and pulled it in five holes.

'It's a bit big for me but then I've got a very small waist,' she said comfortingly. I hated her thin bottom-less figure. Anyway, my dog made a pool on her carpet, which was strangely comforting.

I got asked to a Hunt Ball after Christmas. Christmas time, as every girl worth her weight in horseflesh knows, is Hunt Ball time. The weediest weed you've ever seen asked me to one. I accepted because my mother said, you never knew who you were going to meet, and he might have friends. She always says that about weeds. Either he might have friends or he's a UP (Useful Person). My mother knows lots of UPs. She doesn't particularly like them, they're just useful.

This weed was a small long-haired thing with suede shoes. When I met him at the station he was wearing one of those Tyrolean hats with feathers and badges stuck round the band. With his silly chinless face underneath he made me panic, he really did. I was quite polite to him to begin with, but he went to sleep after a bit and snored with his mouth open. It was a nice day so I hummed a bit and felt quite happy.

When we arrived at the other end the weed woke up, and a scarfed lady in trousers met us at the barrier. She looked quite human for a horse.

'I'm glad you managed to catch that bloody train,' she said, and while the weed was putting the suitcases in the boot she said, 'Has he been a bore?'

I nodded.

'Yes, he always is,' she said, and winked. Quite a jokey lady really.

This Horse had a very beautiful house. It was Tudor with a super long drive, and smelling like an antique shop inside: lots of uncleaned ancestors and medieval toothpicks on the walls, and huge cold bedrooms. We had tea in the drawing-room, sitting miles apart from each other and balancing scones on our knees. The Horse talked away in a loud voice with her feet apart, and ate sandwiches in one swallow. There was another boy besides the weed, a tall fair-haired type called Michael, in an expensive suit and a watch-chain. The Ball was being held in a place called Elkerthley Castle. Pronounced Elly. It's a game all that stuff. Churpoughlin equals Chulin; Smith spelt Smiffe. You can't win.

I changed, jumping up and down, dressing with one hand and rubbing myself to keep warm with the other. The Horse came and fetched me to go downstairs. She was wearing horse harness, or regulation pink for lady horses at Hunt Balls: halter neck, scraggy bodice and skirt hanging saggy from the waist down. She told me a bit about who was coming.

'The Boddington Smyths, very well known in the County, some very good hunters, the Scudderburns, no stable to speak of. But quite nice. Sir Henry and Lady Piltwhistle, Jane and Miranda; and Nigel Denthead to make up the numbers.'

Michael and the weed were in the drawing-room when we went in. The Horse gave us all drinks, and I talked to Michael who wasn't swoony but better than the weed any day. Weeds get frightfully possessive when they take you to dances. They go on as if you're engaged to them or something. Always looking at you or passing you peanuts and getting absolutely furious if you dance with someone else. I think they think that when they pay for your ticket they've bought you for the evening. It makes me nervous. I keep thinking everyone else is thinking I *mean* to be dancing with a weed, when I don't at all. It's just my mother's hoping he'll have some useful friends.

Sir Henry and Lady Piltwhistle arrived with Jane and Miranda. The Horse introduced everyone, Nigel Denthead was announced, and we went into dinner.

I sat between Sir Henry and Nigel Denthead.

'Do you hunt?' Sir Henry asked as he sucked at his soup.

'Occasionally,' I said, because you couldn't be too careful.

'You'll be at the meet tomorrow?'

I grunted into my spoon. I wasn't going to be if I could help it.

'I'm following on foot. My mare's thrown a spavin.'

'Ah,' I said, but I'm not with it spavin-wise, so he turned to Mrs Boddington Smyth and started discussing spavins with her.

I listened to everyone else during the fish. Mrs Scudderburn was being enthusiastic to Mr Boddington Smyth. She had a funny face. Not the sort that would be enthusiastic to everyone. And throwing her bosom all over the place as if no one else had one. Nigel Denthead was talking to Lady Piltwhistle, poor woman. If horses had their own saints she'd be Saint Piltwhistle first class. I bet when she was pregnant she knitted four bootees instead of two.

'Where do you live?' Nigel Denthead turned his great shining face towards me.

'In London.'

'Not at the weekends too?'

'Why not, I live there.'

'Interesting,' he said. 'Tell me - what does one *do* at the weekends in London? I've always wondered.'

I looked at him. Damn flunkey. My grandmother always says damn flunkey, especially about bank managers. I gave him what she calls a 'look'.

He didn't look flattened by my look. He just went on being shiny and eating his chicken.

I turned back to old Sir Henry. He was discussing the price of manure with Mrs Boddington Smyth. There was a man who knew which side his dung was buttered on. On the other side of the table the weed was talking to Miranda Piltwhistle and giving those chinless *wuffs* weeds always give when larfing. I turned back to Nigel again and asked him where *he* lived. It was that or manure.

After the coffee the girls stomped upstairs to powder their noses. I went up to Miranda Piltwhistle in the loo. She was doing her hair. She had this fuzzy fair hair and small eyes. I can't stand fuzzy hair and small eyes. One or the other, but not both.

'I love your dress,' I said, 'I've always wanted a net dress.'

She put on her lipstick in the mirror.

'You should get one.'

That was the end of that conversation. I didn't care. I hated her dress, not even a horse would have been seen dead in blue net.

Elkerthley Castle stood on top of a hill. It was pouring with rain so you left your car at the bottom and there were Land-Rovers to take you up. Everyone brought wellingtons to change into before getting in the Land-Rovers. Jane Piltwhistle got left at the bottom because she couldn't find her wellingtons. Not surprising really, because I had them on.

The beginning of a Hunt Ball always follows the same routine. All the ladies troop off and leave their coats in the loo, and on coming back spend a pleasant half-hour searching (nose to wind) for the gentlemen who have hidden themselves in the bar. My luck was way out that night. I bumped straight into old Nigel Denthead. Was he pleased! He beamed at me and grasping my arm with one wet hand steered me on to the dance-floor.

Dancing with a weed is worse than talking to one. That's what hell is going to be like. It won't be torture and groaning, it'll be dancing with a weed for ever and ever. I bet the devil won't be tall and evil, I bet he'll just be a complete weed with wet hands. And when you jive with a weed he just stands throwing you about, and looking smug while you kill yourself. That's another thing about Hunt Balls. There you are in long dresses and tiaras and you're supposed to dance like a beatnik. The band plays away at all these Charlestons and things, and you dance like a fiend looking a nit with all these petticoats and things on.

I'd only been dancing with Nigel for about a quarter of an hour when Michael came up and asked me to dance. I was so grateful to get away I practically burst being charming to him. We went to look for some orange juice, then he took me down to this night club they'd made in the dungeons. It was meant to be terribly sexy with candles and a crooner groaning away at the microphone. Actually it wasn't at all sexy. Just pitch-black, so you couldn't see if you were dancing with the right weed or not, and damn cold. I jumped up and down to begin with, but after a bit I couldn't even feel I had any legs, so I stopped. I think Michael was probably cold too actually, because we went upstairs after half an hour.

The Horse had hired a private room for the evening. When we found it Nigel and the weed were getting drunk there. Not funny drunk, just boring drunk. Michael went upstairs for some more champagne, and I sat on the sofa. When he came back, he said the cabaret was about to start. Nigel stopped being drunk and straightened his white tie. This *was* his big moment. He was in the cabaret. He was going to do a super solo playing the bagpipes. We all followed him downstairs to the main hall.

I didn't take much interest in the cabaret until old Nigel's turn came. With a big smile to all of us he put the pipe-thing to his lips. Good old Nigel! Sweat poured off him. We waited for a wail, but not a squeak. Then like a balloon deflating he sank slowly to his knees in a dead faint, and the bagpipes with him. He was revived with a soda-siphon, and I gave him a glass of brandy to cheer him up. He was the only amusing thing that evening, he really was. The Horse was disgusted. Didn't speak to him again that night. Said he'd let the Scots down.

The rest of the evening was pretty boring. Just dancing away with one weed or another, to keep warm more than anything. Then it was bacon-and-egg time. That's the only thing that's good about Hunt Balls, the bacon and eggs at five o'clock. I suppose it's psychological really, because it means no more weeds for that evening.

Nigel and the weed had a duel on the way home – with champagne corks. They had proper seconds and everything, but neither got hurt, unfortunately. Nigel only gave the weed a small black eye, and the weed missed, so it wasn't much fun. The two Piltwhistle girls came back and had coffee. Nigel kissed Jane in the back of the car; even she didn't look too thrilled.

We didn't get to bed till about six o'clock. Then I was practically sick when I saw hunting stuff laid out in my bedroom for me. I used to be madly brave on a horse when I was about thirteen, but since I'd been going to dances I'd given up horses in favour of weeds. Less dangerous really. And a weed will at least take you to the movies, which is more than you can say for a horse. However, I couldn't think of a good excuse not to hunt, so I just thought, if you've got to, you've got to, and there's nothing you can do about it, and got into bed – with my fur stole pinned round my legs.

A nice maid woke me up at nine o'clock. She was a bit surprised to see me wearing my coat and fur stole. But she agreed it was the only way to keep warm. She helped me into breeches and boots and tied my stock for me. The boots were a bit big for me, so I stuffed them with tissue paper. I don't mind telling you I was shaking up and down when I stomped into the stable yard. The first look between you and a horse is the important one. A horse can size you up in a minute.

Everyone else was mounted and ready to move off towards the meet.

'Your animal's tacked up, we'll start off slowly if you'd like to follow,' shouted the Horse.

I looked into all the boxes till I found a rather small square cob. I led it out into the yard looking it squarely in the eyes. It wouldn't stand still while I mounted so I had to hop on one leg half-way down the road before I could get the other one over. That's the trouble with being small: you always get put on small horses, and they're much more energetic.

The meet was being held at the local pub. They handed round steaming punch, and everyone looked happy except me. I chewed a piece of chocolate and did up my girths. The Horse came up.

'Shorten your reins and stick behind me, and you'll be all right,' she said, 'and if you must come off for heaven's bloody sake come off after old Denthead.'

The field moved off and I followed Mr Boddington Smyth. He was a coward, thank goodness, and went through a gate when he thought no one was looking. Then the hounds lost the scent so we sat around and munched sandwiches and talked to a few of these nutcases that follow on foot. They're potty. No honestly, I think they're really nuts, people who follow hunts on foot. They stomp all over the countryside just to see a few horses' behinds disappearing over the other side of a hedge. Then they go home quite happy. That's all they want out of life, just to see a few horses' behinds. Then they die quite happy. Some of them even do it twice a week: not only on Saturdays; they sometimes do it on Thursdays too. Just stomp, stomp, after these horses' behinds.

We moved off again, and we were going really rather well when old Boddington Smyth pulled up suddenly.

'There he is!' he shouted. 'After the bastard!'

'Who?' I asked.

'Bloody anti-blood sports snoop! Taking filthy photographs again! Bloody Socialist. After the brute, we'll have his blood!'

He plunged his spurs into his horse's sides and I followed him.

The little anti-blood weed saw us coming and started running towards the road, his camera bouncing up and down. Then he fished a bicycle out of the hedge and peddled furiously up the road, his mac flapping in the breeze. We would have lost him if his mac hadn't caught in his wheel and practically strangled him. I thought it was jolly bad luck. I didn't think it was fair to throw his camera in the pond after that. But Boddington Smyth wouldn't listen, and he wouldn't let me help the poor thing unstrangle himself. He said he was to be left there to rot. I don't know if he's still there, I really don't. It was quite a deserted bit of country so he might be.

The Horse was thrilled when I told her. She said it was the nicest thing she'd heard for ages. Made her day. When I said it was a bit unfair to leave him to rot, she said what did I want to do, tuck him up in bed with a kiss?

4

Migo and I were quite glad to get back to Paris. Migo hadn't met a superman during the holidays. She'd collected a few new weeds but nothing much to speak of. I hadn't either actually. I went to see my old actor once in his dressing-room. Migo came with me. We took quite a long time trying to decide whether it was chasing someone to go and see them in their dressing-room, but in the end we decided it wasn't. I wanted to look frightfully *femme fatale,* so I wore a black dress and a black ribbon round my neck. The bodice of the dress was rather big for me, so I stuffed one or two of my father's socks down my bra to make me look bosomy. Sort of earth-mother appeal I thought. Migo said she thought sixteen was a bit young to develop earth-mother appeal. But I said the Italians were like that when they were sixteen. She said I wasn't Italian.

I was hell's nervous in spite of those socks to boost my bust. It was all right during the play, and in the intervals I had a few vodkas, but when it came to actually walking round I kept on thinking of why I shouldn't go. The stage door man looked very leery when we asked to see him.

'You needn't look like that,' I said in a sort of bored voice, 'He's a friend of my parent's.' But he was unimpressed.

I couldn't bring myself to knock on his door. I kept on dashing towards the fire escape. So Migo did it for me.

He looked very sweet, this actor. He really did. With holes in his vest. I think holes in a vest can be very endearing. There was this other woman there too. I think she was in love with him too. But I wasn't jealous. I bet she loved him because he was amusing and handsome. I bet she didn't think once about him having an innocent smile. She probably didn't think like that at all.

Anyway, he talked more to me than he did to her. I'm not really a bitch, but I couldn't help feeling triumphant, because she was at least twenty-five. She kept on giving me great looks, really as if she could have killed me. It was a good thing she didn't know about my father's socks, she wouldn't half have mocked me, honestly she would.

I made a big resolution not to think about him in Paris. It's perfectly feeble to go swooning round the place about someone who isn't there, and anyway isn't swooning over you. Besides being very boring. I did keep a small bottle of scent he gave me when he was in Paris though. It was one of those samples you get given sometimes. I asked Migo and she said it wouldn't be cheating to keep it. So I did. Every now and then I had a look at it, but mostly I was quite good.

We found Paris just the same when we got back. A bit more beautiful, because it was beginning to be summer. There were tons of bronzed Scandinavian types at the Sorbonne. Marvellously blond and healthy and shining white teeth. Funny thing though, because someone told me that if you actually go to Scandinavia none of the people who actually live there look like that. It's just a front they put up when they're abroad.

My mother said I had to learn to cook. She's keen on cooking and things, as I've told you. I asked around where the best place to go was, and someone suggested a cooking-school just off the Boul' Mich. Migo and I went along and enrolled for ten lessons, every Monday and Wednesday. There were about six other girls doing it with us. Well, at least they weren't all girls. Some of them were quite old and married. There was one American woman whose husband was going to divorce her unless her cooking improved. She was very sad about it. He was in the army, stationed just outside Paris, and she said he preferred eating with the men to eating at home. She had pebble glasses and enormous feet and gym-shoes, so I don't think her cooking was the only reason.

We had to wear nylon overalls, and everyone was given a different course to cook. Migo had to make strawberry ice-cream and I had to do *pot-au-feu,* and this American woman had to do savoury tartlets. They sound pretty simple. But they're not when you've got an old French hag shouting at you. This American woman had to roll out her pastry nine times, and then when she started putting the savoury on to the pastry she was so short-sighted she made neat little piles all over the table instead of on the pastry.

Migo's strawberry ice-cream was no picnic either. She had to grind away for hours at this eighteenth-century strawberry crushing machine. That's the thing about French cooking; they never use anything that hasn't been around for at least fifty years. And they never wash their saucepans. That's why everything has a better flavour in France. No, honestly, there's nothing like hygiene for making things tasteless. And, if they buy a Hoover, they carry on about how marvellous it is, then go back to using a broom. They're traditionalists really.

I felt quite happy about my *pot-au-feu*. It just meant cutting up millions of vegetables and chucking them into a saucepan and leaving them.

When everything had been cooked we had to sit down and eat it and discuss it. People said pretty feeble things, because it's jolly difficult to think up things to *say* about something you've seen being dropped round the floor or scraped off a stove.

I was still feeling happy about my old *pot-au-feu* when I went downstairs to fetch it. Then I had a taste. It was fantastic. All the vegetables were absolutely raw. They'd been cooking for about three hours so you'd have thought they would have been all right. I turned the gas up and tried to boil them a bit more, and poured in tons of salt, but it didn't make any difference. I felt pretty keyed up about taking it upstairs and having everyone talking about it. I thought of dropping the dish on the stairs, but it was too much trouble. Besides, I'd have to spend hours and hours picking up every pea. The French never waste a thing.

I gave them all a big smile when I went in and said,

'I think you're really going to enjoy this.'

Then I went round holding the dish while everyone helped themselves. There was a lull before they began to eat. I couldn't take it. I took the dish downstairs and paced up and down the kitchen, praying. I couldn't hear any screams of rage from upstairs. Then Migo appeared, carrying the dirty plates and screaming with laughter.

'Quick, run before she catches you,' she said, 'she's broken a tooth on one of your carrots.'

I flew, tearing off my nylon apron, with small green recipes floating from the pockets. I know I shouldn't have. It wasn't chivalrous. I should have stayed and done the decent thing. But I couldn't have afforded to pay for a Frenchwoman's tooth. Teeth are terribly expensive in France. Honestly, they cost a fortune.

We had to find another cooking-school after that. Not such a good one, but they didn't ask for *pot-au-feu*. Migo said it didn't matter about that woman's tooth because it was only a back one. I said, was she sure it was a carrot that broke it, and she swore it was. Rather funny really because you'd never think a carrot could break someone's tooth. Migo said it was probably the way I cut them up.

A huge dark-haired weed called Jeremy rang up one evening and asked me to go out with him. I'd met him at a dance during the summer. I thought he was quite nice then. He'd told me all about wanting to be a monk. I think he must have forgotten about it. I was watching at the window for him the following morning, when he came chugging into the courtyard on a motor-bike. I'd never known a man who went about on a motor-bike before. He had one of those hats and goggles and everything. He took them off and did his hair in the mirror of this motor-bike.

When he came up to fetch me, I introduced him to Madame. She thought he was swoony, because he spoke this marvellous French. It really was brilliant actually. And there's nothing the French like better than someone speaking marvellous French. I didn't listen to his French much though. I just kept looking at his head. He had frightfully smooth brown hair all plastered down, except for one bit that stuck straight up in the air like a flag at the back of his head. It kept on waving about as he talked. I don't think Madame noticed because she was swooning, but I couldn't take my eyes off it.

After a bit of chat with Madame we went off to lunch on his motor-bike. I sat side-saddle at the back, and he put his hat on again, so I couldn't see this bit of hair. But when we got to the restaurant he took it off, did his hair all over again and left the same old bit sticking up. I wondered if it was his personal aerial. I made myself stop looking at it during lunch. It's no good letting a bit of hair ruin your lunch. We talked a bit about what we were going to eat, then I said,

'That's a jolly good motor-bike you've got.'

He looked as if I'd hit him.

'That's not a motor-bike,' he said. 'It's a Vespa. Don't you know the difference between a motor-bike and a Vespa?'

I said, no I didn't, and he spent the rest of lunch drawing engines on the tablecloth. Then he trundled me off to the Champs Elysées, where he was taking part in this Rally. It was just about to start when we arrived. There were millions of Vespas all decorated with garlands of flowers, and practically every nationality in national costume sitting on them ready to go up the Champs Elysées. It was very gay, it really was. I didn't mind Jeremy's bit of hair or anything. I just chatted away with all these types. Then a super-looking Italian came up and asked me if I would sit on the back of his Vespa, because the girl he was meant to be taking felt ill.

It's very heady stuff driving up the Champs Elysées on the back of a Vespa, kissing your hand to the cheering crowds. When we reached the top I got off and a gendarme sat me on one of the traffic lights. I couldn't stop laughing. I had that fantastic feeling when you're going to burst any minute. You just feel you could pick up everything and take a bite out of it like a piece of cake. Great slices of sky, Champs Elysées, gendarme. Everything.

Jeremy was frightfully peeved because I hadn't gone on the back of his Vespa. Actually I never found out what the point of the Rally was, because we went off to tea and never rejoined the others again. I was sad because I liked that Italian. I expect he was pretty boring, but you can't tell if you don't speak Italian. Even 'pass the butter' is exciting if you can't understand what they're saying. I went on going out with Jeremy after that. But after a bit I really couldn't stand it. It wasn't only engines the first couple of times, I mean he was really interested in them. He really liked the way engines worked and how fast they went and everything. Madame was frightfully disappointed when I stopped going out with him.

Mostly because he kissed her hand, and spoke this wonderful French. I tried to explain about the engines, but she didn't understand. He didn't talk to *her* about engines.

Of course the French absolutely hate the English. They just pretend to be swoony about them so they can spend their summer holidays in England. And once they are in England, they're a dead bore. No really. There's nothing you can show them they haven't got better in old France. And they spend the whole time writing air-mail letters and reading piles of French magazines. Then when they go back to France they carry on forever about how *'sensationnel'* everything in England is. And pretend they had fantastic romances with men the dead spit of the Duke of Edinburgh.

Madame had a huge cleaner called Madame Genevieve who loathed the English. Ever since she spent a month in Eastbourne when she was seventeen. She said she'd never recovered. She used to lie in wait for me every morning pretending to wash up while I ate my breakfast. She always said the same thing to begin with:

'Quand j'étais à Eeeesstbourne...'

Then we'd be off. Every morning we went from *croissants* to Agincourt. She said everyone knew that the only good thing in England was *le cardi anglais* and *le duc d'Edinbourg*. Honestly. She couldn't even admit that English loos were better than French ones. She said they were just different. She said, '*la coutume est differente, c'est tout*'. I'll say.

As the weather got hotter Migo went on a lot of these coach trips to stately homes that her club organised. She loves clubs and evening classes and all that. Honestly, she'd join anything. I once went to a keep-fit class with her. It was terrifying; huge women with fantastic muscles skipping about in swimsuits doing dainty gym swinging clubs and skipping ropes and pointing their toes all over the place. I nearly died I was so embarrassed. Migo loved every minute, she said it did her good psychologically. She came out feeling a new and better person.

She took me on one of these stately home coach trips once. I went with her and this other friend of hers called Birgitte Applestrohm. She was quite a girl, old Birgitte. Very sexy. You could see she was. Even if you were a girl. I mean, often men swoon and you just can't see what they're swooning about, but you could with Birgitte. Migo said that she had great hordes of clean American lovers. Very clean and white-toothed with big chests, Migo said they were. She brought one of these types with her on this coach trip.

We started off early with a picnic lunch, and I wore a straw hat. This American kept on pushing it on to my nose. He thought he was being really funny. He didn't only do it once. He kept on doing it, and then splitting his sides. I got a bit fed up I can tell you. Then Migo and I were munching away at our sandwiches during lunch and he came gambolling up with Birgitte and practically sat on top of us, under this tree. It gave Migo indigestion them being under this tree.

'They think they're the latest thing from Zola, full of milky bosom and hidden desire,' she said to me. 'Elma's giving her sun-kissed embraces.'

'You're just jealous,' I said.

'Oh yes, I'm green,' said Migo, 'I can't wait to lie laughing in the arms of a blond beast with a crew-cut, capped teeth, and a popcorn busting out of his pockets.'

We walked round the gardens after that because Migo was getting a bit cross. I knew what she meant actually. Too clean people make me feel pretty strange. They're not like people at all; they're like vegetables wrapped in cellophane. They don't look like vegetables at all. I once went to stay with some people whose daughter married a friend of my cousin who happened to be there when they got back from their honeymoon. They were both bronzed and very beautiful, and her mother kept purring on about how marvellous they looked together. And how ecstatic they were and all that. But do you know every time I looked at them, I'm not really joking, I felt peculiar. They were *so* beautiful they didn't care about anyone. Not even each other. They were the sort of people I imagine old Hitler would have swooned over.

If you want to know about old Birgitte, she had to marry that drip. Migo said she didn't want to, she just thought she ought to. Pretty depressing having to marry someone because you're pregnant. I think she got to regret those sunny kisses.

I don't think I'll ever have to marry anyone actually. 'Course you can't be absolutely certain about anything, but I don't think I will. My family don't tend towards sex really. I don't think I do either. I mean I find it frightfully difficult to take sex seriously. No honestly. I think it's terribly difficult to take sex seriously if you've got a sense of humour. If you think of any sex maniacs you know, they haven't got a real sense of humour. They've got a sense of fun all right but not a real sense of humour. The tendency in my family is drink. My brother hasn't got it; I have but he hasn't. When I was at school I kept vodka in my tooth mug. And once at a house feast I got pickled on cider because I drank all the prefects', and no one was ever allowed to have it again. They had to put me to bed singing 'God Bless the Pope' at least that was what it sounded like.

The worst I ever got drunk was when my brother came to see me in Paris. He turned up one evening with a very relaxed friend. He was the most relaxed man you've ever met. He was so relaxed at Cambridge he got sent down. Anyway, they were feeling very extravagant because they were only in Paris for the weekend, so we rang up a French bird and arranged to meet her at a cinema in the Champs Elysées. She was very pretty this girl. And very smart. The boys brightened up like mad, and I did too. No, really I did. I like pretty girls, they're much easier to get on with than ugly ones. I suppose it's because they usually have a better time.

The movie we went to see was very sad and beautiful. It was the sort of movie that makes you feel lonely inside. Like when you're in love. You feel all gone inside and empty. That's when you get this Tendency, because you just make for a bottle to make you stop thinking about this all gone inside feeling. Anyway, I had this feeling from seeing this movie so when we got to the restaurant I started to drink. It was the perfect place, because there were Russian fiddlers and everyone else was pretty tiddly and singing and laughing. It was the sort of place you want to dance a wild fandango before you've been there a minute. We had a few vodkas to begin with, and toasted the Tsar. It was splendid except for the French girl.

She wouldn't drink a thing. She sat looking very po saying she'd just have a lemonade. My brother's friend thought she was sweet. I didn't. I thought she was a drip. I can't bear people who won't be super and wild when you should be. I started talking to everyone and singing. 'Course the more po this girl looked the more wild I got. You know how you do, if someone disapproves. Luckily the boys joined in, so she faded away into a corner until we were very, very tiddly indeed. When we got out of the restaurant she went home by herself in a taxi, and we tried to think where we'd left the car. But this relaxed boy kept on saying to my brother,

'Your sister looks just like Gertrude Lawrence.'

And we'd all stop thinking about the car and scream with laughter. In the end we got a taxi and went to look for the car. We couldn't find it, so we went to the boys' hotel instead. They went upstairs to get something, and I sat in the hall and waited for them. There was an old woman trying to persuade the man behind the desk to let her take a boy with her upstairs. I think she was going to seduce him. Anyhow the man wouldn't let her. I didn't blame him. She was screaming drunk and foul. I went to the mirror and did my hair. Suddenly I looked from her face to mine. It was awful. Honestly, I looked as beastly as she did. I thought, I'll end up like her. It starts off like this. You get drunk because you feel all gone inside, then you end up like her. Probably worse. Lying in a gutter somewhere with people spitting on you. I've never been tiddly like that again. I've often wanted to be, but I haven't. Tendencies are no joke.

I'll tell you another thing that gives me that all gone feeling. Strauss waltzes. You know, when I dance one of those waltzes I think I'm going to die. Only I don't, I go on living, and that's much worse. My last evening in Paris I danced one of those waltzes with the Count. Then we walked round Paris for hours and hours. Pretty corny I suppose. But I wanted to remember Paris exactly as it was then. Then, when I was seventeen. So that when I'm eighty and crippled with age and disillusioned and bitter, I'll have Paris to look at as if I'm seventeen. Disillusion and bitterness won't matter. I'll have one huge beautiful thing to look at without sadness. I've often wondered if you could do that with a person. Just remember them as they are when you love them most, and keep that in front of you and never notice when they're ghastly. 'Course there's always the risk I won't get embittered. But it wasn't a risk I could take with Paris.

I stood and watched the dawn break over Paris from the Sacré Coeur. Even the Count shut up. It was unimaginable. Cold and silent. And the sky like – I don't know – heaven, I suppose.

5

When I got back to London, my mother said I had to do a secretarial course. I wasn't too pleased about that I can tell you. I said I didn't want to do a secretarial course. And she said, well, what did I want to do? I said I wanted to be 'discovered'. She said, doing *what?* So I did a secretarial course.

My real trouble is I'm absolutely normal, and I've got no ambition. Don't think I feel all right about being normal, because I promise you I don't. I don't go about being smug about it, honestly. It's not just now I'm normal. I mean I haven't just begun to be normal. I've been completely normal my whole life. Honestly, ever since I was born.

I suppose it began when I was born. First of all I was completely healthy. I wasn't purple, and no one was worried about whether I was going to live or anything, and my mother didn't hate me. It would have been all right being healthy if my parents hadn't wanted me, but they had. That was a bad start. Then when I got a bit older I was good-tempered and had a good appetite, and did perfectly normal things like running away from school. It's been a great burden to me. Being normal. And I've never had a neurosis, no really, not one. And no complexes either. So that's why I submitted to doing a secretarial course. And if you want the truth, that's the worst thing about doing a secretarial course. Having to be normal. And going round with everyone else who is being normal and doing a secretarial course too. It worried me no end, going round with these normal people. But I didn't do anything about it to begin with.

My mother knew about me being in love with this actor, but she didn't do anything about it until one evening when we were alone. Then she began to ask me what happened in Paris. I didn't know what to say. When people talk about things they seem to distort them. Everything gets boiled down to motives or generalised. You just feel an enormous cliché: the eternal young innocent in love with the older man. And it's not that at all. You know you're the old, old story, but that's not it. You're not really innocent, he's not really old. It's just that he's perfect.

Anyway, after she'd hedged about a bit, I said,

'Oh well, I suppose I'm in love with him, but it doesn't matter, I'll get over it.'

She gave me a worried look.

'Don't you think it would be a good idea to try to forget him?'

'Why?' I said.

'I could tell you why, but I don't want you to be disillusioned.'

'It's all right, I don't mind being disillusioned. I don't *like* being in love.' She paused then she said,

'He's going to marry that girl he's acting with at the moment. She saw him off at the airport when he came to Paris, didn't he tell you?'

Then suddenly I could hear time rushing by me. Honestly, it sounds stupid, but I could hear myself talking and watch myself. You know like when you're drunk sometimes.

'You mustn't be hurt, darling,' she said, 'men love young girls because they're innocent and flattering.'

'Oh,' I said, 'I didn't expect him to take me seriously. I just loved him. Stupid really.'

I didn't cry, I just went to bed. I didn't mind about him going to marry that actress, I just minded about her seeing him off at the airport. Honestly, that was the only thing I minded about. It just made when he was in Paris seem like nothing. It probably was nothing to him. He was probably yawning his head off.

But I remembered that I'd rushed into his arms and laughed and shouted and practically broke his hand holding on to it. I couldn't believe it was him, for heaven's sake. He probably gave that pottery thing we bought in Montmartre to his old actress. Honestly, you feel a fool when you think about things like that, because you really think they're perfect. Just nothing wrong with them.

I believed her though. My mother, I mean. But I still had to go and see for myself. I was pretty nervous because I always was when he was about. His flat was at the top of a long staircase, so when the maid let me in all I could do was pant. The room was full of sunlight, and he was in bed with 'flu or something, and there was another man there. I stood looking at them, panting and shading my eyes. He said hello and introduced me to the man. I sat on his bed and talked to them for a bit, and this other man kept asking him how he was every five minutes. He had a photograph of his old actress on the wall. She looked quite pretty. I didn't mind. I just minded about him probably having given her that pottery face.

I looked at him when he was talking to the other man, and he wasn't perfect any more. Just a man in bed with 'flu.

The other man went, and he said,

'Can you see my cigarettes?' I had a look around and couldn't, then he said,

'I think they're under the bed.'

So I bent to pick them up and my knees cracked. They always do, I used to lose five marks every ballet exam. Anyway, he pretended not to notice when my knees cracked, and I gave him the cigarettes and said,

'I think I'd better go. I'm meant to be at a lunch.'

And he said,

'I'll ring you up and ask you to a movie one evening.'

And I said,

'Yes, that'd be super.'

And I walked out into Mayfair feeling rather relieved actually. He wasn't perfect any more. I wasn't in love any more. I suddenly realized I wouldn't have to be nervous or feel like hell any more. Not ever again. Then I thought: What am I going to *think* about? What was I going to wish for? I couldn't think of a thing.

Perhaps you don't understand, but you've got to wish for something the whole time when you're seventeen. You've got to, or there's nothing to live for. However impossible you've got to *think* you want it. It doesn't matter if it's a superman or a sports car, it's got to be something. Or you want to commit suicide.

When I couldn't think of a thing I wanted I nearly did. I nearly stepped in front of a bus in Notting Hill Gate. I just happened to see a rather cheery dog on the other side of the road, so I didn't.

What with not having anything to think about and doing a secretarial course with all these normal people I was pretty depressed, I can tell you. But when you're depressed I think you should start again. You know. Do corny things like changing your hairstyle, and getting a new lot of weeds. So I changed my hair. I had this enormous beehive. Well, the girl in the shop said it was a beehive, but my father said it was a bird's nest, and I looked better before I went in. He said why pay good money to some old hairdresser, when he could do the same thing for free. He can be quite boring like that. I mean he thinks he's being pretty funny, and my mother thinks he is too. I think he's a bit feeble really. When he goes on like that, I mean. Most of the time he's all right.

When I'd changed my hairstyle and got a few new weeds, I still didn't feel very jokey. So I thought, hell, I'll have a go at being a beatnik. I knew it wouldn't be easy because of being so normal. Also I didn't know any beatniks. I just knew girls who were going to be debs, and they were no use. I didn't look much like a beatnik either, in spite of the beehive. But then I thought I'd be dead cunning. I'd look so like a real beatnik that no one would find out that I was really normal. I knew if they found out I was normal I'd had it.

So okay I'd got a beehive. Now I wanted a jumper. You only need one jumper if you're a beatnik. If you change your jumper you lose your identity. I asked Migo about this jumper. She had a cousin who'd been a beatnik. Or had a boyfriend who'd been one or something. Anyway, she found one of her father's gardening jumpers that he'd been through World War I in. It had a few bullet-holes, so you could tell it was genuine all right. It was very long. Down to my knees. And it had a collar you could pull over your face if you didn't want to see anyone. With my tight jeans and beach shoes, I looked the real thing, I really did.

There was a pretty drippy beatnik in my class at secretarial college. I stood her a coffee and a cheese-cake a couple of times, so she'd help me join the Chelsea Set. It was worth it, because she arranged to take me to a Saturday-night party with a couple of male beatniks. She was really wet this girl, but you can't pick and choose your beatniks if you only know one. She was a bit doubtful about whether I'd be all right, because I looked so normal at college. However, I spun her a great story about my mother hating me, and having to live at home because I'd no money.

She lived in a flat with three other beatniks. She said she was looking for a man to live with. So far she'd had no luck. I'm not surprised actually, because she really was wet. I said why didn't she live with a beatnik? She said it was too expensive. She couldn't afford it. They ate such a lot. And besides, she didn't know any that were house-trained.

I was a bit nervous when I turned up at her flat for this Saturday-night party she'd asked me to, in case she'd tell me I looked too normal to come. I pulled my jumper up to cover my nose, so only my eye make-up could be seen, and rang the bell. I'd been practising this hop up and down that I knew beatniks did, and I started to do it when she opened the door. Then I sort of slid sideways up the hall corridor. She looked quite approving so I think I was quite good at it.

These two male beatniks were in the drawing-room when we went in. They were sitting on the floor. At least one was sitting on the floor, and the other was behind one of the armchairs. Me and this girl sat on the floor too. Then she introduced me to the one sitting on the floor near us. He was called Webb and he wore these monk's sandals. I don't think he washed his feet. It didn't look as if he did anyway. He didn't talk much either, just sort of grunted. I don't think he was in a talking mood. After a bit we crawled round to talk to the other one behind the armchair. He was called Spence. He wore these really round gold-rimmed glasses. He was much worse than Webb. And he was frightfully sweaty. I mean his shirt really stuck to him. I don't swoon over men who sweat a lot, I really don't. Nor does my mother. She's always thanking God my father doesn't sweat. She says she doesn't know what she'd do if he did. You know, some men have only got to start talking to you and they start sweating and taking out their hankies and mopping themselves every two minutes. This beatnik Spence, he was that type. Really sweaty.

After we'd talked to Spence for a bit, we thought we'd go to this party. It wasn't very far. Just round the corner from this girl's flat, so we walked. It was terribly windy, which was maddening, because by the time we arrived I looked really healthy. Honestly, blooming and rosy. I nearly killed myself, because I'd spent hours putting on this green powder I'd bought. I mean, except for being normal, looking healthy is the worst thing that can happen to a beatnik. Even if you're abnormal as hell and shaking with neurosis, if you look healthy no one's going to believe you. Luckily I'd bought some dark glasses so I put them on and they covered most of my face up and my jumper covered the other half of it. So no one could really make sure that I was healthy.

The party was in the garage of one of those small mews houses. You know the kind. It was pretty crowded by the time we arrived. I mean, people were beginning to stand on each other and things. They don't usually start standing on each other till it gets crowded. Not usually. I crouched by the wall, while Spence went and got me a drink. That's the first principle about being a beatnik: if you don't know anyone you mustn't let on. I mean you mustn't *look* as if you don't know anyone. If you're alone you must look as if you're thinking, or brooding about your mother, or something. Don't for heaven's sake look as if you'd like to talk to someone. Talking to someone, I mean sort of chit-chat about this and that, is strictly for the birds. So I crouched by the wall as I was saying, till Spence came back with the drink. I sunk my head right down, and twisted my legs in a faintly Yogi-type way. A little bit of Yoga or Zen Buddhism is very useful. I'd seen a programme on television about Yogis so I knew a bit about it.

When Spence rolled up with a bottle of wine I pretended not to notice him. It's quite a good thing not to notice people. Anyway, I pretended not to notice him, so he began to scratch. Honestly, I don't know what his chest was like but he made a noise like a nutmeg-grater. Backwards and forwards, louder and louder, so in the end I raised my head and looked at him. He went on scratching with one hand and handed me the bottle of wine with the other. I gave him a sinister look through my dark glasses and took the bottle and drank. He took it back and had a swig himself. Then he said,

'Man.'

That really bored me. Him saying that. For heaven's sake, talk about type casting. There is a limit. I stood up and leant against the wall and I groaned. I've got a good groan, so Spence looked quite taken with me standing and groaning.

Then he said,

'Let's roll.'

But I pretended not to hear and just went on groaning, so he took my hand and dragged me towards the other end of the garage where people were dancing. I really felt like groaning then. I told you he was sweaty; well, you can imagine it was no picnic dancing with him. He clutched me to his damp shirt and danced slowly up and down breathing heavily with steam rising from him. In fact he never made much progress because he kept on stopping and having to take his glasses off and wipe the steam from them.

Then a girl started screaming. You wouldn't have heard unless you were near like we were. They were really agonising screams.

'What's with her screaming?' I said.

'Her father's just become a duke,' Spence said.

She was in a real state this girl, sobbing and shouting that her life was ruined and things. My father's a corny old lord but I don't let it ruin my life. I mean you've had it if you let things like that get you down.

'Let's go upstairs,' I said.

Spence scratched himself for a bit then agreed. So we crawled across the garage and up the stairs to the kitchen. There were a whole lot of bodies necking on the landing carpet, so it took a bit of getting into the kitchen. There was someone sitting in the sink reading a book and eating cheese. Quite a nice face I thought, but I didn't say anything. I put a string of onions round my neck and lay on the floor. Spence lay on the kitchen table and ate a pear. Then someone came in and said,

'Any of you booked for the bedroom?'

Spence sat up and gazed down at me on the floor.

'You booked?'

I didn't know what he meant, but I said yes, because he made me feel ill. Honestly.

It turned out that the man who owned the house lent his bedroom, and you paid a quid to go in there with some type for half an hour. This really wet beatnik girl went in there about five times. I know I'm narrow-minded but honestly you might as well be a tart. I mean, for heaven's sake, tarts get paid. She even went in there with old Webb and his monk's sandals. Still I suppose I can't judge. But Webb. Honestly, you should have *seen* his feet. Old Spence was a bit fed up with me so after he'd scratched for a few minutes he slid out of the room looking furious. I didn't take any notice. I just stared up at the ceiling.

When he'd gone the man in the sink said,

'Have some cheese.'

It was good cheese so I said,

'This cheese is really mean,' I said in a groany kind of voice.

He agreed, and we went on like that for a bit. I got to feeling better as the evening wore on.

He was really a good beatnik, that man. He was called Herb. And he knew about things. I mean he could read and everything. And he was quite conversational. He talked to you and asked you what you thought about things. Which is very unusual. We talked for a long time actually. He sat in the sink most of the time, and I sat on the draining-board. One thing he said. He said that when you died there were probably only about five people who were strictly really sorry. He said you'd be lucky if there were five. I think he meant other than your relations. He didn't have any relations. Relations usually mind if you die because it means one less relation. It makes them feel better if they've got a lot of relations, even if they don't particularly like them.

After we'd talked about who would be sorry if we died he asked me to dance. I said okay and we went down to the garage. I tried to think about who'd be sorry on the way down to the garage. I mean I started counting them up. I know a lot of people, but I won't tell you how many would be sorry. They'd all go to my funeral, okay, but they wouldn't be sorry.

Herb was a good dancer. I was enjoying dancing with him when old Webb appeared. He flipped towards us in his old monk's sandals. He had a frightfully smug look on his face.

'That bedroom is the most,' he said. He was looking really silly. He looked like someone who has had a really good meal, then tilts his chair with a grunt and looks pleased with himself. You know what I mean. I'd hate it if someone looked like that after they'd made love to me. I really would. I've never slept with anyone. So I can't talk. But a lot of people talk about sex to you. I mean quite old people who are married and things, and some of them make me feel very uneasy. I don't think they can have loved anyone if they talk like that about love.

Herb had a blank face. Not much expression or anything, but I don't think he liked old Webb either because he started dancing again while Webb was still talking. Then I trod on Webb by mistake. So I turned round and said, 'Like I hope your Webb foot's all right,' and roared with laughter. I thought it was a pretty funny joke. Actually I always think my jokes are funny; I'm about the only person I know who laughs when they tell a joke. Really, everyone else keeps a straight face. I don't know when they're making a joke so I spend the time laughing like a maniac in case they get offended. Webb didn't think that joke was funny, so he walked off. Herb did though. You could tell he did, in spite of his having this blank face. He didn't laugh or anything. But you could tell. You don't find many beatniks who laugh actually. They shout and groan and sometimes one or two will make a joke, but it's not often you see them laugh.

We'd just started dancing again when old Spence steamed up. He was really sweating. I mean it was dripping off him.

'Someone's pinched my overcoat,' he said, and he was shaking up and down. All that beat stuff went west once he lost his overcoat. He was absolutely normal. It just shows you. Anyway Herb went off to look for it with him, and I went and asked a girl who was kissing someone by the door if anyone had left. She had these marvellous leather boots on with fur round the top. When I asked her she stopped kissing this weed and said, 'What?'. So I said,

'Where did you buy your boots?' and she told me. She said they weren't very expensive.

It turned out that the only person who'd gone off in a black overcoat was someone in monk's sandals. Good old Webb hitting back at Society again. Spence wasn't surprised. He said Webb had been locked in a cupboard when he was four. His subconscious never recovered. If you ask me he was probably cold.

Herb took me home about six o'clock. I got a fright when I did get in actually. My father was waiting for me. He was green. No kidding. Really green. I mean the colour of trees and leaves and things. He thought I'd been murdered or something boring. He was even more furious because I *hadn't* been murdered. Honestly, it takes a lot to make him happy. Anyway he was so furious, luckily he couldn't speak. It's much worse when he can speak. He gets frightfully witty-witty. That's much worse. Honestly, much.

I went to a lot of beat parties after that. I didn't have to go with that wet girl because of Herb. I got to know most of the beats around Chelsea. Not all of them but most. I couldn't have stuck them if I'd had to go with that girl every time. As it was I had to go on having coffee with her at college. She was so boring. She just went on and on about how many men she'd slept with. I think she was a nymphomaniac. I don't know how you qualify, but I think she was. She was damn boring anyway. I haven't met many, but they usually are. Herb was practically the only person worth talking to at those parties. He was beat all right but he was worth talking to.

Then he got run over. I never found out how it happened. I just noticed he wasn't there. I asked someone after a couple of weeks, and they said he'd been run over. It gave me a bit of a shock actually. No one knew if he'd got buried or anything. He didn't know anyone but beats so he probably got put any old where. You wouldn't catch a beat paying for a funeral. No one minded except me. They didn't even pretend to be sad. That girl at college said, why should she be sad, she hadn't slept with him? I didn't have coffee with her after that. In fact I don't think I spoke to her again. I was sorry I stood her that cheese-cake.

I gave up being a beatnik after Herb got run over. I wasn't in love with him. Nothing like that. He was just nice. Very simple. And I liked talking to him. Beatniks were too conventional anyway. I mean they thought they were getting away from it, which is pretty corny. You never do. You just change one thing for another. I was too fat to make a good beatnik anyway. You have to be thin. No really. You've got to look really skinny or it's no good. Not only your face, all over. Still, it was quite interesting being a beatnik.

6

After I'd been a beatnik I thought I'd have a real change. So I became a deb. I don't know why I became one actually, because I always swore I wouldn't. But you know how you become things, you sort of drift into them. No one really says anything; you just suddenly find yourself doing them.

I started off with one advantage, because of my father being a lord. If you're a deb you've got to be rich or have a title. One or the other. Of course, if you've got both, you're in clover. You can't fail. If you've neither, you might get about a bit. But nothing much to speak of. My mother was quite keen on me being a deb, because she thought it would help me forget that old actor. My father didn't say much. He never does. Except 'how much will it cost?' My brother was keen too because it meant a lot of free parties. People ask him out a lot because they've got this idea he's eligible. No honestly, they really think he's eligible because of him going to be a lord when you-know-who dies.

Actually I don't think I've told you about my brother. He's the only one I've got. I haven't got any sisters, just my cousin who's as good as. I'll tell you something about my brother. Everyone says he knows where he's going, he's got his head on the right way, and all that. But at heart he's a beatnik. He doesn't look like one because of being in the cavalry, but he is. One day he's going to stun everyone and elope with a jazz singer of forty. I hope he does. I would if I was him. He doesn't say much. He's like my father: not a great talker. But I should think he gets fed up with people saying that all the time. Mind you, I don't know but I should think so. I would. Drive me barmy. Mind you, people once they start thinking one thing about you, they never stop. If they say you're just like a great-aunt, they'll go on saying you're like this great-aunt till you're a hundred. It doesn't matter if you change and become completely different, they still go on saying it.

To begin with when I started being a deb we were a bit in dickey's meadow, because my mother's not a flitty Society type. So she didn't really know any debs or their mothers. But I knew one or two girls from school who were doing the season, and some from college. So they soon mounted up. The tea parties I mean. That's how it works. You get asked to someone's tea party and meet all these girls. They take down your name and address and ask you to their tea party, and you do the same to them and ask them to yours. You scratch my back and I'll scratch *yours*. It's quite a good system really. A lot of mothers won't let their daughters go to someone's tea if they don't know them. But that's pretty drippy really, because knowing people's got nothing to do with it. It might have been in their day, but not anymore.

Your mother is a very important bit of being a deb. She has to go to all these lunch parties and chat to other mothers. My mother found luncheon chit-chat an awful strain. She's very intelligent so that kind of conversation got her down. I used to cheer her up beforehand, and she borrowed my grandmother's diamonds and things. But it was still hard work. She was quite amusing about them afterwards though. She said the frightfully rich ones kept their minks on all through lunch. She said they'd rather melt than take them off. And everyone cheered up when they heard I had a brother. The point of being a deb is to get married I suppose, though not many of them do. But that's the object really. So a brother is good news.

Of course doing the season is expensive. It was expensive even for me and I did it on the cheap. I had all my clothes made and bought remnants. We had a jolly funny time actually. You can't help giggling when you go round buying things with 'shop soiled' on them when everyone else is flying to Paris to buy theirs. It was things like tea parties and stockings that cost the most. It was all right if the tea party was near the secretarial college or your house, but if it was miles it cost a fortune. Migo and I used to take the Underground and then get a taxi and arrive looking frightfully respectable. It wasn't so easy going back, but sometimes we'd get a lift. Stockings and shoes were pretty boring though. The thing to do was to put your ladder on the inside of your leg and stick your shoes with Sellotape. It had to be expensive Sellotape because the cheap stuff doesn't last.

Most of the girls were pretty rich. Or if they weren't rich they had godmothers who left them money to do the season with. Or their parents were separated. If your parents are separated you usually have a pretty good time of it because if they marry again it's practically always someone rolling, and even if they don't they spend the time competing with each other giving you presents. Anyway, even if these girls didn't notice the ladders or the Sellotape, you thought they did. You'd chat away to them and hope for the best, but they'd be quite unmoved by jokes or anything. Just stare through you. It's quite daunting having someone stare through you if your shoes are stuck with Sellotape. Most of the time I think they didn't notice actually, I think they were just rather dumb and couldn't think of anything to say.

Even if you had new shoes, tea parties were pretty sinister. You spent the whole time sitting on the floor eating sandwiches and swopping addresses. Most of the girls were nice-looking. I mean *looking* at them was okay. It was just talking to them that was awful. They spent the whole time asking you if you were going somewhere. And if you weren't they'd stop talking to you. If Janey-Lulu hadn't asked you to her luncheon you'd had it. I'm not joking. They wouldn't talk to you for days. If you mentioned anything else they thought you were potty. No really. Nuts. You couldn't blame them really, they didn't know any better. They didn't even know how to begin to talk about anything else. Nor did their mothers. It wasn't their fault.

Tea parties went on for practically ever. Everyone went on and on giving them. If they liked you they didn't only ask you to one, they asked you to about half a dozen. And if there was some bit about you in the newspapers they'd all swoon.

Even girls who you knew hated you. There was this girl at college like that. She really loathed me. I couldn't stand her. Do you know she hated me so much she wouldn't even let me cheat in a short-hand test. Nobody gets through shorthand without cheating. It's never been known. Anyway, when she sat next to me during one of these tests she made me put the book away. Everyone else had theirs out. But no, she didn't, so I had to put mine away. Then when there was a piece in some newspaper with my face on it she practically killed herself being nice to me. She really thought I'd fall for that. For heaven's sake.

Most people give cocktail parties after they've given a whole lot of teas and lunches. Cocktail parties are worse than tea parties. They're worse than dances too, come to think of it. In fact they're the worst thing you could possibly do. Except shorthand. It's all the weeds you have to talk to. They're much worse than the girls. Millions of times worse. If you find the girls chilling you wait and see what you'll find the men. You really get fond of the girls after you've met the men. I thought I knew how weedy a weed could get.

But I didn't. I didn't know even half how weedy a weed could get.

When you start going to these cocktail parties the first mistake you make is to think they want to talk to you. So you go up and start talking. You know, I chit-chat about things. If a weed thinks you look all right he'll talk a bit. Then he'll start asking you where you live and how many houses you've got and whether you're giving a dance. If you've only got one house you're lucky if he stays two minutes. They don't believe in wasting time, weeds. Gosh no. They're off like a streak of lightning. I don't blame them. I don't really. If you only want to know heiresses and stuff it's no good talking to people like Migo and me. It's a simple outlook really.

You develop a technique after a bit. Cocktail party technique. First of all you don't care. Then when you go in and see rows and rows of enemy backs facing you with no gaps to break through, you don't just stand and hope. You dive through their legs and start talking non-stop at whatever you come up face to face with. You talk so fast they don't have time to ask you how many houses you've got. And you *will* them not to walk away. You've got to will jolly hard. Sometimes it doesn't work and they walk off. But you just spring on someone else, and if they walk away too you take a taxi to the next cocktail party. And start all over again.

Of course you meet the same weeds at dances, but it's not nearly so bad. Because they have to talk to you at dinner. And when you get to the dance you don't have to talk to them because you're dancing and you can pretend to be concentrating. It's a funny thing about debby weeds actually. None of them are rich or eligible or anything. In fact most of them are absolutely broke, and not a title between them. You'd think they would be because of all these heiresses swooning over them. But they're not. One man I knew quite well was a complete rotter. He didn't pretend not to be. I mean he told you that he was, which I think was quite fair. These girls' mothers paid him to take their daughters out to dinner. He said it brought in quite a steady income. And he never had to pay for anything. Tax-free too. Which isn't to be sneezed at. He had this double-barrelled name he'd made up, and he used to tell them he'd made it up and no one believed him. They thought he was joking. There's a book printed for these debby weeds listing all the girls coming out and their hobbies and how many everything they've got. So really it's a pretty good sideline. And dead simple. You've only got to have a dinner jacket, reference books, and a tennis racket for weekends and you're in business.

Loos are very important during the season. I should think they're practically the most important bit of the season for some girls. I know one girl who did her whole season in the loo. She used to take this small edition of *War and Peace* about with her in her evening bag. She got through it seven times in one season. She was quite a slow reader. Migo had a copy of *Gone with the Wind* she hid in the loo at the Dorchester, so she just curled up with it till it was time to go home. They couldn't go home straight after dinner because their mothers would be furious and say they were failures. It's one thing to be a failure. But it's a hell if your mother keeps telling you. And some of them could go on for hours.

My brother was quite keen on all these parties to begin with. But he soon got bored. Pretty soon I can tell you. He's quite intelligent. Very intelligent actually, so debs rather got him down after a bit, after the novelty wore off. He found it was impossible to remember their names, because they were so long. And he said, even when he did remember their names, they all looked the same. So he gave up going after a bit. Except if it was a relation or something.

Country dances could be fun though. Honestly, get a weed among green foliage and pastures, and he wasn't nearly so bad. Some of them even became quite human. Made jokes and things. You usually stay the weekend with someone for dances in the country. The people who give the dance fix you up with someone who lives near. You really had a nice time if the people you were staying with were fun. It didn't even matter if the dance was bad, you could still enjoy yourself, because you had all these trees and things to look at. Even if you were bored you could enjoy the view.

It was nerve-racking if you got taken to the dance alone in a car, especially if it was a long drive. The thing is you nearly always got told who you were going with and there was nothing you could do about it. You can't tell some po old hostess you don't want to go with someone because he's a sex maniac, and being raped by a weed would be no joke. I'm not exaggerating: some of those weeds, there was nothing they wouldn't stop at. Mostly because they're so stupid. No intelligence at all. So they get bored. They really live with boredom all the time. That's the reason they're so nasty most of them. They're just so bored. Nothing to think about or anything. Just dance after dance. Anyone would get nasty being bored all the time. Honestly, even a saint.

My mother used to get very cross. About these types asking if they could rape you all the time. She said they didn't go on like that in her day. She said they always brought you chocolates and flowers and you went to football matches, but they didn't rape you. I don't think she knew the same types actually. I mean, the summit of her season was the Cuckfield Hockey Dance. She was a simple country girl, so I asked her what I should do about these rapey sort of weeds. She couldn't decide whether I should learn driving or have a police whistle. In the end she settled for a pepper-pot. She made me keep this pepper-pot in my evening bag. So if a weed really leaped on me with a low growl all I had to do was open my evening bag, get out the pepper-pot, unscrew the lid and chuck the pepper in his eyes, in one easy movement. Migo and I practised once and it was impossible. It would be all right if you knew when they were going to leap. Then you could start undoing your bag and unscrewing the pot beforehand. But you don't. And when it was damp weather you couldn't even unscrew the top because it got all clogged up. You were really in dickey's meadow.

It wasn't only the weeds that could be nerve-racking. Some of these snobby old girls were pretty frightening. I mean girls' mothers and things. The thing is, in theory you think, pooh I'm not frightened of some old bag. But it's no good pretending because no matter what you do you still feel jolly nervous. I used to try anything. All the old gimmicks, like imagining them with nothing on and all that, but it didn't help much. You weren't always frightened of them because they were frightening, or you felt shy, or knew they were going to ask you something ghastly. Often they just frightened you because they were so horrible. Not frightening horrible. Just horrible. I'd never met people so heartless. Mind you, I hadn't met a lot of people. Though even now those smug women give me the creeps, and I'm getting on. No chicken.

I had a dance of course. And a cocktail party and everything. Rather good. I thought so anyway. I don't think my father was amusing though. Most of the time he talked to the maid downstairs. Drips and stuff aren't really in his line. He'd rather be in the kitchen with a bottle of whisky. When I said why didn't he have a go at talking to some of them, he just said,

'I'm damned if I want a whole lot of weeds in my hair.'

He isn't bad at talking to people once he gets down to it. He puts on this very pally expression and they tell him practically anything. Nearly every party there he is with this pally expression listening to some dope and them telling him the secrets of their hearts. I don't think he wants to hear the secrets of their hearts. He's just got this face people tell things to. Honestly, they just see his face and make straight for it. Poor old boy. I think he gets a bit bored sometimes.

After I'd had this dance, being a deb tailed off really. I went on being one officially till the end of that year. But I didn't feel like one much. I didn't feel like anything much. I just felt like someone who has been a beatnik and a deb, and rather bad at both. I didn't know what to be or anything. I didn't want to go on being a deb because I wasn't much good. And I didn't want to be a secretary. So I just kept going to all these parties to stop thinking about anything at all. Honestly, if you don't want to think you just have to keep going to millions of parties and you don't have to. I've never seen anyone thinking at a party. I'd have noticed if I had.

My mother was thinking though. Mostly I think she was thinking what to do with me. After a bit she decided I ought to do this model course. To make me more dignified. And to learn to sit down properly. She's very keen on me sitting down properly and my legs looking tidy and things. I don't think they ever will be actually. I don't think she thought they would either, but I suppose it was worth a try. Also I've got these thick eyebrows. I think they got her down.

The first day I went I had to go and talk to a man. He saw what sort of shape I was, so I suppose he guessed I wasn't going to be a model. He asked me if I was shy. I said, no, I wasn't shy, but my legs were untidy. He said they could probably tidy them up. He said they tidied most people's up after they'd been doing this course for a bit. He said he'd seen much worse than mine. Honestly, he said they were quite mild compared to some he'd seen. I was quite cheered I can tell you. You are cheered, you know. If someone's seen legs worse than yours.

All the other girls doing the course were very thin and tall. I was the only one who wasn't. But they were nice. Thin but jokey. They were all going to be models except me.

The first day we had to walk up and down. It sounds easy as anything. But try walking up and down with fourteen thin girls watching. Normally when you're walking you don't think much about it. It's only when you start walking up and down in front of someone you feel loopy. Like when you start thinking about your ears. Day-to-day you don't think much about your ears except to hear through them or something. But when you actually think about an ear, and its shape and what it looks like and the way it's stuck on your head you feel a bit of a nit about it. It's exactly the same when you start walking up and down in front of someone. You suddenly realise you've got two legs and feet on the end and knee-caps and things. It's a bit much.

Practically the whole of a model course you spend walking up and down. When I did it I tried to make jokes so people wouldn't look at the way I was walking. That's all you can do really, make jokes and hope for the best. If you're my shape and you've got my legs. Actually even the thin girls felt loopy walking up and down. They were very good at laughing at my jokes which was nice because they weren't very good jokes.

They also make you walk up and down in front of a mirror and watch yourself. And look at your shape. When I was looking at my shape in the mirror, the woman said,

'You're pear-shaped.'

So I said,

'I had hoped I was hour-glass.'

But she said no. I had to face the facts. I was pear-shaped. I was a bit depressed because I hate pears. 'Specially their shape. Still, if you are you are. Even if I was an old skeleton I'd still be pear-shaped. I expect if someone digs me up in hundreds of years I shall be known as 'the pear-shaped Kensing-dearthal woman'.

There was one super woman who gave us choreography. You do choreography to break down your inhibitions. She liked me because she said I wasn't inhibited. She said it didn't matter about your shape if you were uninhibited. She said people forgot about your shape. Also most of the pear-shaped women she knew were uninhibited, so perhaps that's the compensation.

We spent quite a bit of time putting on make-up and trying out different shapes for our mouths and eyes. It was rather interesting. A lot of people, when they'd finished, you wouldn't have known they were the same person. And without any make-up on at all you wouldn't have recognised any of them. Apparently that's the whole thing about models. They're not meant to have faces. In fact, if you want to be a model, it's no good having a face. If you've already got a face you can never look different. If you haven't got one then you can paint a new one on every other day if you want to. That's why I'd have been no good even if I wasn't pear-shaped. Because I've got a face. Honestly, I've got practically every disadvantage you can have. No really. You name it, I've got it.

After we'd spent two weeks walking up and down and breaking down our inhibitions and putting make-up on, we had to bring our clothes to model. All different clothes. Sports clothes, day clothes, evening clothes, everything. I had a pretty embarrassing time with sports clothes. I brought a pair of trousers and a silk shirt to model. And I'd just started modelling them when the woman stopped me.

'I didn't tell you to bring jodhpurs,' she said.

'They're not jodhpurs, they're trousers,' I said.

'They don't look like trousers,' she said, 'they look like jodhpurs.'

'It's the shape of my legs,' I said, but I was very embarrassed I can tell you.

We had to model with an umbrella as well. I kept on stubbing my toe and putting it in the wrong hand, and the woman got furious. She said I was doing it on purpose. When I glued up my eyes with eyelash glue, she said I did it on purpose. I didn't want to glue up my old eye, I'm just no good at putting eyelashes on with my right hand. I'm left-handed. They never stopped me being left-handed at school, in case it made me more backward. If you're backward already, changing hands could make you retarded practically your whole life. It could even affect the way your brain worked.

The last day of the course we had to put on a show and be given marks by a panel of people. It was pretty funny all these people trying to put on polite faces at all these really mangy clothes everyone was modelling, and pretending not to notice my being pear-shaped. The choreography woman was one of the panel, and she gave me huge winks to cheer me up.

In the end I got quite good marks, which practically killed me. They said I had a good smile, and being pear-shaped wasn't counted against me. They said I couldn't help it.

So there I was, an uninhibited pear-shaped ex-deb with a good smile. I suppose there's worse things to be.

7

Of course I hadn't stopped thinking about a superman. In spite of being a deb and all that. When I got
depressed I used to think about that actor. And once
when I was attacked by a sex maniac. It's not much fun
being attacked by a sex maniac. I can think of more
swoony things. It's not the bit when he leaps on you,
or the bit when you try to run and your legs don't
move. It's the awful way you get haunted afterwards.
You keep on thinking *everyone's* going to leap on you.
No really. Once it gets dark every man you see seems
about to. When I was running away from that old
nutcase I kept on thinking about that actor. Mostly
because of this innocence he had I suppose. Like you
think about something beautiful in the dentist.

When I got really dismal I used to sit around
and think I'd probably never meet anyone like that
again. I thought I'd probably end up being a spinster.
And everyone saying poor-dear-it's-a-very-Sad-Story
she-was-disappointed-in-love. You know how they

do. Or I thought I'd probably have to be a maiden aunt. Actually I could never decide which was worse, being a maiden aunt or marrying a weed. If you don't find a superman that's about the only choice you've got. Or being an eccentric. I think I'd go in for being an eccentric if I didn't find a superman. I'd wear a straw hat and live in the south of France. Sometimes I think that'd be better than marrying a superman and becoming disillusioned. People's faces go so funny when they're disillusioned. Their eyes go all small and they spend the whole time thinking someone's doing them out of something. And saying I'm-not-such-a-fool-as-I-look-oh-no. And waving their fingers in your face.

Anyway, though I didn't have a superman to swoon over I had a good collection of weeds. The one I liked best was this terribly rich one. I hate to think about it now but I really did like him. I mean it's no good pretending I didn't like him because I did. You get all these girls who fall in love with drips, find out they're drips, and then go round swearing they weren't in love with them, they just felt sorry for them. I wasn't in love with this rich weed; he just amused me. I think I liked him best because he was the richest and he had this oil well. And he thought being rich was a joke. It's no good having an oil well if you don't split your sides about it. That's the trouble; most people take them frightfully seriously. They really think it's frightfully serious being rich and having an oil well.

I've forgotten where I met him, this rich weed. Anyhow, he used to take me out quite a lot. My grandmother thought he was swoony. Anyone rich is swoony to her. No, I'm not being mean. That's just how she thinks. I mean, she doesn't *only* like rich people, she likes poor people too, but rich people have this particular appeal for her. She liked it when he sent me huge bunches of flowers and presents. She said that was what she understood.

We spent a good deal of the time drinking champagne. I thought you could never get tired of drinking champagne. But you do. Everyone swooned when I drove up with him. They wouldn't have swooned if I'd come by myself. It was the oil well they were swooning about. I know it's corny but I never realised till then that people really minded about money. Not really cared for it. But they really do. It doesn't matter if you're some frightfully rich fiend in human shape; if you give them a big tip they'll smile and practically kiss your feet. I think it's a bit frightening. Because supposing you become a fiend, if you're frightfully rich, no one tells you, and you just go on being a fiend till you die. It makes you think.

Old Cecil – he was called Cecil, this rich weed – was on his way to being a fiend when I met him. But I didn't notice it at first. Of course he didn't have a chin or anything. But when you've been a deb you don't expect people to have chins. I mean a chin is a rare luxury. Not something you come across just like that. And the thing is, if you use your imagination, you can pretend they've got chins. And Cecil could be amusing. At the beginning anyway when I hadn't heard any of his jokes. When I was hearing them the second time round it wasn't so easy to imagine he had a chin. That often happens to me actually. I think someone's really amusing; then when I've been out with them a couple of times I realise they've just got these four or five jokes they tell you, and that's all. Except for these jokes they're hell's boring.

What got me down about Cecil in the end was him telling me about his mistresses and looking flabby. I can't bear chinless people talking about sex. I think all chinless men should be eunuchs. I don't mind if they propose to me, that's quite jokey-jokey, but when they look all flabby and start telling me about their mistresses and talking about sex I want to nun. I couldn't stand it when Cecil went on like that. I used to start talking to the waiters or the people at the next table or something. Once when he just wouldn't stop I sang.

I think I went on going out with him because I didn't like to disappoint my grandmother. She really enjoyed thinking about the oil well and everything it was selfish to stop. But it was really torture in the end. He became more and more of a greedy pig. He didn't care about people building all over England, ruining it. And when I got angry he said, didn't I want to house the workers? I said, they just care about the workers, only their bank balances. And wearing their diamond bracelets at lunchtime and stuffing their faces with pâté. For heaven's sake, you can't eat more than three meals a day.

You can keep your old oil well and yachts, and everything. My grandmother thinks I'm mad. No, honestly, mad. 'Specially when I stopped going out with old Cecil. She said she couldn't understand it. When I said his chin got me down and he made me feel sick when he talked about sex, she said that sort of attitude wouldn't get me anywhere.

I got a temporary job when I left secretarial college. My brother said I needed the experience.

The thing was I owed him a whole lot of money. So he was pretty keen on me getting experience. I found this agency and they took me on because they didn't have anyone else. They kept on only giving me half my wages by mistake, but they were quite jokey so I didn't really care. Also they said I was their best girl so I felt rather sorry for them.

They sent me to this place that published hymn-books and encyclopedias. They were good hymn-books actually, and you could buy them on the HP. I shared a room with a woman called Miss Watts, and a Greek boy. I had my own typewriter and typed things on cards with numbers on them. And Miss Watts used to dictate into this tape-recorder and I typed back from it when she'd finished. I was really meant to be working for this man behind a partition, but whenever he wanted me to do something Miss Watts said I was too busy.

It was a tight fit sharing a desk with Miss Watts. But she was quite interesting. She had a brother who grew vegetables and one grandfather who'd been a Mormon. She wasn't a Mormon, she said she couldn't be doing with all those husbands. Because of only having a one-room flat. The Greek boy and me thought this was terribly funny. He had to add up things in books, and if he wanted a bit more money he just took a frightful long time adding up and got paid pounds and pounds for working overtime. When I left he gave me a pair of pink garters with bows on. Miss Watts was thrilled. She said it was the most romantic thing she'd ever heard. I gave her a box of chocolates and she gave me a handkerchief with a dog on. Only she cried so much I had to lend her the dog back to wipe her eyes.

The reason I left was I was meant to be going to stay with this girl in the south of France. Also I'd paid my rotten old brother back his money. This girl was an International Set type. I don't know why she asked me to stay. I think she liked me because I wasn't. It made a change me not being a princess or anything. She had this terribly good-looking mother she absolutely hated. She said she wouldn't have minded her being a drunk and having lovers if she was nicer. But she didn't even make her laugh.

They had a pink villa and Italian servants like on the movies. And lots of princes and kings staying. That was another thing. This girl's mother was mad on kings. Honestly, you'd only got to say you were a king and she'd swoon. She wasn't too keen on me not being in oil or being a princess, but she put up with it. We spent most of the day on the beach or water skiing, and then in the evenings we went to night clubs after dinner. They were pretty grim. Nearly all the men had bald heads. No honestly. When you looked round all you saw was bald heads everywhere. Even girls my age were dancing with bald heads. A lot of them were married to them too. Apparently their mothers sold them to the first rich lech that came along. My girl-friend, she was terrified she'd get sold too. There was this American who kept on asking her to marry him. He didn't have a bald head but it wouldn't be too long. And her mother was dying for her to marry him. She wasn't in love with anyone else but she didn't want to marry him. I mean I know supermen end up with bald heads but it's pretty stiff starting off with one.

I met an Italian prince while I was there. He was called Carlo. Actually I've never met one that wasn't called Carlo. He wasn't amusing, but he amused me. He was typical old Roman playboy type. The sort the old Borgias chewed up for breakfast. Anyway, I used to dash about in his sports car with him, and he took me to the casino and places.

But it was hell if you were on the beach with him because he had these huge biceps. And he did noth-ing but flex them all the time. He thought everyone on the beach was probably swooning about his old muscles, so he stood about flexing them and then walked up and down frightfully slowly swinging his hips in one of those men's bikinis. I practically died every time he did it. I used to hide behind the lilo and pretend I wasn't with him. But then he'd come and stand in front of me and breathe in and out very slowly. I think he thought I was probably swooning too. If I pretended not to notice him he'd dive into the sea and swim up and down with a snorkel on. He was really embarrassing. Most of the time he was all right though.

One thing about the International Set, they're like beatniks. No one's normal. I suppose being a king and things is a bit of a strain. And Oedipus and all those chaps were pretty royal. I mean it's not often you get peasants being in love with their mothers or obsessed by anything in particular. They swoon over old nymphs flitting about woods and things but it's not often they're incestuous. Anyway I shouldn't think you could go round with the International Set if you were normal. It's no good just being in oil or being a princess; you've got to be perverted or obsessed too. Not only that, you've got to be bored stiff at being perverted or obsessed. It's no good enjoying it. 'Course if you're a princess, in oil, perverted and obsessed, you're in clover. You can't fail. It's not often that happens. Sometimes, but not often.

Another thing you've got to be perverted in the right places, like Montego Bay or Cannes. It's no good doing anything like that in the wrong places. There's practically a special date when it begins. Like grouse shooting or anything else. You know: 11th March, incest begins. Also no one at your school should have been normal. Unless they were all complete nutters your small talk will be nil. You can get over that though if your butler's really a woman. It's not as good, mind you, but nearly.

I got on quite well with these kings actually. I think it was such a change me being normal. No really. I think they were fascinated because I was normal. 'Course I didn't stay long enough for them to get bored of me being normal. They probably would have.

When I got home my cousin went off to be a nurse. It was pretty lonely her going off. I missed her a lot. She's good company and everything and we shared a room at school and all that, and once she was a nurse I never saw much of her. She's the sort of person you like to be with. I mean she laughs all the time. I like people who laugh all the time, you get jolly few girls who laugh a lot. They're usually too busy taking their sex appeal seriously. They take their sex appeal so seriously they hardly ever think about how funny everything is. Especially their sex appeal. That's the funniest bit of all.

She used to do this thing, my cousin. Mostly when we were at school. Though once she did it when we were staying in a hotel. She used to make me cover my mouth in lipstick, and she would too. I mean you had to really smear it on. Then we divided up the mirror into two halves and gave it huge kisses, and then we'd see whose mouth was the biggest. She always won. I think that's why she played. And on bath nights at school we dressed up as tarts or Grecian statues. Never anything else because when you've got just sheets you're a bit limited. Unless you're Julius Caesar. And it's not much fun being Julius Caesar. I mean you can't do much when you're Julius Caesar. Except drop dead or write long letters home from Gaul about woad.

We were never jealous of each other because we were so different. It's frightfully boring when you get people being jealous of each other. Particularly if they're jealous of you. I mean *anything* you've got they make you feel guilty about it. For heaven's sake, they make you feel guilty about being alive. There was a girl I was a deb with, She like that. If she came to see me, she'd spend the whole time counting my invitations or my dresses or something. I think that's the only reason she came. She never talked to me till she'd finished thumbing through everything. Then if I'd got a single thing she hadn't she'd be ready to kill me, or look terribly sad. I can't bear that. When people go all droopy and sad. I know it's phoney because as soon as they get what they want you don't get a drop out of them. My mother does that sometimes. She doesn't get furious and shout, which is quite all right. She goes all quiet and sad, especially when you owe her money.

Anyway, after my cousin was a nurse I didn't have anyone to dress up like a tart with. Not that I wanted to particularly. It's just nice to be able to just in case. I suppose I could have had lipstick competitions with someone else, but it's not the same thing really. I don't know why it isn't, it just isn't.

It happens all the time really. I mean people going off and doing other things. Or they become completely different. That's worse. I mean it gives you an awful turn. One minute there they are gay and funny and the next time you see them they've become absolute gloom-pots. Except people who become nuns: they always look much happier. That's the sign of some-one holy. Not long faces and laughing. Like the girls at school who spent their whole life in church, and were always the first to live in sin.

I worked in a pool when I came back from the south of France. It was a pool belonging to a chem-ical firm. The pool is where they put all these girls to type. You all sit in rows and there's an old woman of about forty who sits and watches you to see you're working. We all had these tape-recorders, so you typed with earphones on. I really enjoyed it. It was like one of those old movies with Cary Grant. And he sees someone fabulous typing away in the pool and marries her and gets a promotion. All the girls were frightfully nice, and lent you things. And if you made a mistake you just said, it wasn't you, it was the girl who was away.

They didn't even mind when they found out that my father was a lord. A lot of people mind terribly. They become awfully peculiar with you, or they spend the whole time asking you if he eats or has a bath, or if he's even been on a train. And when you say yes, he does have a bath, and he spends most of the morning there reading the Flutters, they don't believe you. Or they hate you. No honestly. They hate you before you've even opened your mouth and they hate you doubly more than they hate anyone else. If you're working for them they get much more furious with you than any other person because they think you think you're superior to them. They really think you *think* that. There's nothing you can do about it, because they think it before they even *know* you. And if you do anything like making a joke or looking happy, you're thinking you're better than anyone else. Honestly, you've had it from the start.

But none of the girls in the pool minded. They just went on being exactly the same. Me and the girl who sat next to me called Deborah used to play jet fighters with our earphones. I'd be Neville Duke and she'd be someone else and we'd make jet noises and do Morse code on our typewriters. It wasn't a very intellectual game but it helped to make the time go quicker. And when the supervisor shouted at us we'd pretend not to hear and make extra loud jet noises. I was sad to leave that chemical firm. It's funny the places you feel sad to leave. But I enjoyed those earphones.

After that I went to work in this advertising agency. I was secretary to someone different every week.

Everyone in advertising is ex-something. Ex-actors, ex-artists, ex-writers, and quite a few ex-people too. There's two things they all mind about: the Client and Sex. It made me pretty depressed all these people being ex-something. I'd rather someone was a bad writer in one room than thinking up sexy ads for morons. I'm sure his wife wouldn't but I would. 'Course if you tell people that, they think you're boring as hell.

There was one young man I liked in this advertising agency. He was really nice. No, honestly, it wasn't sex, he was just nice and intelligent. We used to have chats about books and things. Everyone thought he was flirting with me or something. You can't even say hello when people are sex-conscious and you're in bed. They just don't admit to anything *not* being sex. They don't want anything not to be sex. I mean they practically *die* if everything's not sex. And they practically kill themselves with boredom if you talk about anything else. So if they see you talking to someone they don't want to think you're doing something and not getting a thrill.

I don't think anyone liked me at that advertising agency actually. I can't think of anyone at the moment who did. I don't know. But I think it was basically because I wasn't interested in sex. It's always going to be a disadvantage. Me not being swoony about sex. Most people are. And they don't like it if you're not. I don't know why. I mean I don't mind them swooning. It's just I can't swoon myself. Except if you're in love. That's different. But most people who swoon about sex aren't in love. And a lot of people who say they're in love are really swooning about sex. Serious stuff.

When I'd finished at that advertising place Migo and I went and sailed at this place in Sussex. It was my mother's idea. She's got this great thing that you should always do everything. She never stops thinking up new games she thinks I should play. In case I get asked and can't play them. She has nightmares about me getting asked to play things and not being able to. So now I can do practically everything badly. I can even play Chinese cribbage. No one else can.

Migo and I went sailing with this man with a beard. He was very nice. A lot of men with beards are. My mother doesn't like men with beards. She says she doesn't know what they're hiding and it makes her nervous. Also she says imagination boggles what must get stuck in them. You don't know what you might not find there. Anyway that's what she says. I don't know that I agree with her.

We had long conversations with this man with the beard. About practically everything. It's rather splendid. Sailing along in the sunshine talking about Freud and things. I was no good at sailing. But my mother doesn't mind if I'm not good at things. Just so long as I can do them. She says people have it over you if you can't do things. She says they sneer at you behind your back. I don't mind if people sneer at me. But she does. My grandmother says that's what happens if you sleep with a man. They've got it over you.

Also just after that one of our castles got emptied. It was sold when I was about nine but most of the stuff got left there. So anyway they sent it over for us to sort it out. It was quite a sight. You try emptying a castle and putting it in a dining-room. It's funny how quickly it goes. I mean one minute there are castles and footmen and coronets and all that, and the next there you are stomping about among lavatory brushes and coroneted napkins and that's all that's left. It gave me a strange feeling. Because when you see all your castle sitting in your dining-room you jolly well know that everything like that's finished now. And if you don't realise it's all finished now, you've had it. You get weeded out. No honestly you do. I know lots of people and they just can't cope because they don't want to realise it's finished. They won't let themselves realise it.

There were lots of miniatures of ancestors with serene expressions. It made you wonder what it must have been like then. Because they never doubted they were marvellous. And of course owning so much stuff only made them think it all the more. Actually my grandmother's like that. She's absolutely sure she's better than a whole lot of people. Not in a nasty way at all. She's just quite sure about it. No one's like that now. I mean no one's even sure about the whole world being better, for heaven's sake. I suppose it's old-fashioned to be sure.

8

I've a fixation with Japan. I've never met anyone else who has. I don't know where I got it from. I once asked my father if we have any Japanese blood. He didn't seem to think so. He said you didn't get much Japanese population in Western Ireland. He's a bit Buddhist my father. Very philosophical and all that. Anyway my mother asked this Japanese poet who lived in Paris to dinner once. Honestly, he was something. He talked about being madly Zen, which I knew about. On account of being an ex-beatnik. And he did all this Japanese painting on silk and arranging one flower on a bit of bark. Actually most Japanese people arrange things on bark I suppose, but he was the first one I'd had dinner with.

After the Japanese man had been to dinner he wrote and asked me to have dinner with him; we went to a Chinese restaurant in the King's Road. He chose all the food. All really genuine Oriental stuff; no Americanised dishes. It was very interesting of course, but I prefer the ordinary old sweet-sour this and that and bean sprouts. Mind you, my mother says I'm the sort of person who'd rather eat Tacky Snack pies and tomato ketchup than anything else. My father's a bit like that. He's always having bread and dripping when my mother's not looking.

Anyway we had this dinner, and talked some more about Buddha and cherry blossom. There is quite a lot to say about Buddha and cherry blossom. He told me about his father who was a Buddhist scholar and then he asked me to come and listen to a record in his flat. I said all right because it seemed a bit rude to say no. Half-way there I did begin to get a bit nervous though. It was in the taxi really. He didn't look so inscrutable. I mean I think I did know what he was thinking about after all.

He had one of those terribly quiet flats. With lights over the pictures and a deaf housekeeper somewhere. I sat on the sofa and he put on a record and asked me to dance with him. I didn't want to in the least. I like dancing, but not just by myself in someone's flat. Well, not with a friend of my mother's anyway. Besides he was quite old. I suppose for one glorious evening he'd forgotten he was.

I didn't want to hurt his feelings. I mean I thought perhaps it was an old Japanese custom to dance after dinner. But I said I thought I'd like to listen to his record for a bit first. And then maybe dance later. So we sat and listened to this record. Him at one end of the sofa and me at the other. Then he said, could he recite me one of his poems? So he did, and while he was reciting it kept on moving closer and closer till I was practically flattened against the side of the sofa. Then he said I was like a cherry blossom blowing in a spring breeze. I said, what gave him *that* idea, and he said he'd thought it ever since he'd first seen me. He said he supposed he couldn't ever hope that the cherry blossom could be his, could he? I thought not. I really did. To tell you the truth I was nervous, not to say worried. It can be a bit worrying with only a deaf housekeeper about. I mean you can't help thinking, supposing he tries to pick the blossom for himself?

We had a bit of an argument about me being a cherry blossom. I said I thought the cherry blossom's mother might be anxious about her. He calmed down a bit then. My mother's no laughing matter some-times, so it helps every now and then to mutter about her if you're a bit in dickey's meadow. He looked very sad when I pretended to worry about my mother. He said it would always be the tragedy of his life that I was forbidden fruit. It seemed to have come on autumn suddenly. I said, yes, it was pretty tragic. So anyway, little forbidden old me got in a taxi and went home. My mother shrieked with laughter when I told her. She'd warned me about Japanese etchings; how was I to know they would turn into just the old jazz – with Brubeck? Still, it's all good experience.

About this time they all got into a bit of a thing about what sort of a job I should do. They said I had to settle down and do a proper job. Only no one could think of what I could do. Mostly because of me not being very bright. There aren't many jobs about for girls who aren't bright, and no good at shorthand. I mean I can do it. But I'm no good at it. The thing is most girls are either bright and don't do shorthand or dumb and marvellous at shorthand. It's not often you get girls who can't do anything like me. And when you do, jobs for them are a bit limited, I can tell you.

What I did was to go to all these agencies and they gave me jobs to go and see. But, you see, it was the same thing everywhere. They wanted you to be either clever or good at shorthand. It was a bit depressing. I mean you feel a bit of a failure when no one wants you. Not that you blame them not wanting you. I mean, if I interviewed me, I don't think I'd want me either. In fact I'm sure I wouldn't. Most of all what's wrong with me is I talk and make jokes. I can't help it. It's a nervous habit with me. Every time someone asks me what I like doing or what I can do, I start making jokes. Psychologically I suppose it's because I'm trying to cover up that I can never think of anything I like doing, let alone anything I actually *can* do. I can only think of things I'd like to do if I was someone else. Not many people want to know about that. Not when they're looking for a secretary or something.

Anyway it makes you pretty depressed really. Feeling a failure. You just go on and on seeing all these people. You can feel they don't like the look of you and they say polite things about getting in touch with you later. And however you dress you're wrong. If you wear a camel-haired coat, they think they don't want a dreary bag like you in their office and, if you look smart and with it, they think it might be danger- ous to have a tarty piece among the files. You can't help wondering what it must be like if you had a sick mother and really needed the job. Not being clever or good at shorthand you'd be worried I can tell you. I was only worried because my father was getting a bit bored of paying my bills and me being a failure. And I didn't have a sick mother or anything.

It would have been all right if there had been another failure in the family. You could just say you took after them, but all my family aren't failures. I was the only one. That's the worst thing about being a failure, being alone. My father says it's the same thing when you're a martyr. You're alone. You feel such a ninny being tortured all by yourself. It's not so bad if you're singing and holding palms with lots of other martyrs. Being by yourself is the worst thing.

I've forgotten how many jobs I went for. Millions and millions. Anyway, then I went to this one which was a woman who wanted a secretary. She was a pretty funny-looking, very tall woman, quite jokey but with these very glittery eyes. Anyway, she hadn't talked to me for five minutes when she said she'd have me. I was pretty flattered I can tell you. When you've been practically everywhere hoping people will like you, you're pretty flattered when someone likes you after only five minutes. I thought she was probably terribly acute. My mother couldn't believe it. She was really thrilled. She thought at last I was going to stop being a failure.

The job was helping this woman run a shop in Hampstead for these different kinds of writing paper. She was in charge of the shop, and also there was one other man. I had an office and my own typewriter and telephone. Pretty important. And the woman was terribly nice. She was always coming in and having little chats with me, and I arranged the shop in a different way and she said it was the best it had ever been done and I must have an artistic nature. I'm a sucker for people telling me I'm artistic. Honestly, you've only got to tell me I'm artistic and I'll be their friend for life. I never believe anything else people say to me, only when they say I'm artistic. I suppose it's because I'm not and I'd like to be.

I had to take a bit of dictation from this man as well. He was pretty ghastly. I mean even if you felt sorry for him, but he was still ghastly. You know what he looked like – he looked like a monkey with one of those hanging upper lips. And he used to suck it after every comma. His lip I mean. Honestly, all the time, comma, suck, comma, suck. It got you down it really did. He was terrified of this other woman. I couldn't understand it. Every time she went into his office he'd start scratching and shaking all over the place. Even when she rang him up he'd start shaking. I thought he was nuts. I mean, this woman, there was something funny about her, but she was quite jokey most of the time.

They had salesmen selling suitcases full of samples of this writing paper all round the country and at the beginning of every month they'd stomp in and go over all their stuff with the man and this woman. They waited in my office till she called them in. You know what. They went on just like that nutty man, shaking up and down and chain smoking. It really got me down seeing these men twitching all over the place. And all they'd got to do was have a little chat and go over their stuff with her. After a bit I asked one of them why he was in such a state, and he said it was because this woman hated men.

I didn't think much about this woman hating men. I just thought I was lucky being a girl, because I didn't have to twitch every time she spoke to me. In fact she became nicer and nicer to me. Really lovely. I'd never worked for a woman before who was so nice. She took me shopping with her and had coffee with me and everything. I couldn't get over it. I thought at last I'd found my vocation in life.

It was swoons all round till one afternoon when I was helping her count up all this writing paper and check it off on a list. I couldn't understand why she kept on bumping into me. And then laughing. I mean, there I was humming away counting up all this stuff, and the next minute she'd bump into me from behind and give this funny laugh. Then we were in this large cupboard under the stairs counting up more of this stuff and she started pushing me into these piles of writing paper, and her eyes looked all starey.

Do you know it never clicked till then. I told you I was dumb. I mean she'd got these funny eyes, but nothing else. Lesbians aren't my subject. I suppose it was rather funny actually. Her chasing me round this cupboard and all these stacks of writing paper. I found it a bit difficult to laugh though. What I did do was, I dashed out of that cupboard and locked myself in the loo.

Of course after that she was absolutely foul. I realised some lesbians are the same as men. I mean if you refuse to sleep with a man he's always terribly rude to you. And I realised why all those men twitched all the time. I asked one of them why he didn't leave. But he just said he couldn't, he didn't think he'd find another job. He was dumb like me, and also he was fifty and had three children. He said she knew that. That's why she could be as nasty as she liked. I don't think anything but bad of her. If you'd seen those poor dumb salesmen twitching you would agree.

What happened in the end was that she sacked me the same time as I gave in my notice. My mother was furious. The thing was, I was back where I started. Being a failure again. And it can be pretty nerve-racking having a failure maping round the house. I couldn't tell her about this old girl being a lesbian, because I didn't want to talk about it. When something like that happens I can't talk about it for ages afterwards. I don't know why I can't, it's po-faced of me. But I just can't. I was the same when that sex maniac leaped on me.

I didn't start looking for another job. We were all too bored about me being a failure to be able to think about it for a bit; I started writing this really dull novel. I used to wear this red flannel nightdress to write in. I couldn't write a word unless I had this nightdress on. That's what I did practically all the time. Write this corny novel or spend hours looking at myself in the mirror. No honestly. I spent hours and hours looking at myself and having long conversations with myself. Well, it wasn't always just with myself; sometimes I'd pretend I was talking to someone else. Most of the time I just talked to myself though. You probably think I'm nuts. But I know millions of people who spend a lot of time talking to themselves in mirrors. It's not only me that does it. Actually I still have conversations with myself walking along the street. It can be pretty lonely walking along the street and you don't notice it so much if you have a conversation with yourself. The time goes much quicker.

I was in the middle of writing this novel when I met a swoony man at a party. It was one of those literary parties where everyone spends the whole time asking you if you can write. And you spend the whole time telling them the plot of some corny novel you're writing, and then they tell you the plot of the corny novel *they're* writing. That's all that happens. It's just everyone going round telling each other their plots. I was in the middle of listening to someone's plot when I noticed this neck. I think you can tell what a man's like just by looking at his neck. This neck was pretty good. And so was the man actually. He had a Grecian nose and very brilliant eyes. I suppose those sort of eyes are old hat. But you know the kind that look at you. I mean you really know they're looking at you and no one else. Most people's eyes could be looking at anyone. It's unusual when people look just at you.

He wrote scripts for movies, this man. He didn't tell me about them, but I think they were good scripts. We went out to dinner after this literary party. Honestly, he was fascinating. I mean once he started looking at you you'd be all mesmerised. Say you were taking a mouthful of soup, if he started looking at you, your spoon would get stuck. Absolutely frozen in your mouth. You didn't want to be mesmerised but you just were.

Once he took me to a concert at the Festival Hall, and I felt extraordinary sitting next to him. He kept his eyes on the orchestra and you really thought he was going to turn them to stone. I used to wonder if he had an aunt who was a witch. It wouldn't have surprised me a bit if he'd been a black magic dabbler. It really wouldn't. He was very imaginative of course. I mean he could talk away and interest you and he had a chin. It's marvellous going out with a chin when you hardly ever do. Also when you were with him everything was very exciting. Even walking along a road. When you walked along a road with him it was really exciting. Not just exciting but sort of vital.

You couldn't fall in love with him though. He was fascinating, but you couldn't love him. You were mesmerised. It was a good thing actually, because it turned out he was married.

I didn't know he was married. He didn't tell me for ages. It didn't shock me. Him being married. I think he wanted it to. I don't know why. It was the way he told me somehow. Actually I was steaming up his car window and drawing faces on it when he told me. So I went on steaming it up and drawing faces. Then I just said I didn't think I could go on going out with him. He said, 'Why?' So I said it was against my principles. I've never found out what principles are exactly, but, if I've got any, not going out with married men is one of them. I've got one girlfriend I don't think has ever been out with someone single. She says married men are more mature. They understand her better. Also they're more experienced. Anyway, old married boot was a rotter. Not fundamentally decent. It was a good thing I wasn't in love with him. I might have been mad about him. I mean it wasn't his fault I wasn't.

I was a bit preoccupied with weeds actually. I suppose it was because I wasn't working or anything. You get a bit one-track-minded. Everyone's got to be mad on you or you nearly die. The thing is you keep hoping that one of these weeds will turn out to be a superman. There was one man: I thought he was a superman for three days. Honestly, I was swooning about him for three days. He rang me up all day long and we used to talk for hours and hours. It really got my father down. I don't know what he'd have done if I'd been mad on him for more than three days. It was pretty embarrassing when I wasn't mad on him the fourth day actually. I don't know why but suddenly I just wasn't. He asked me if I loved him in a coffee bar, and I said yes, with my fingers crossed under the table. I don't think it's a lie if you have your fingers crossed. And I couldn't say I wasn't. I really couldn't. Not when I'd been mad about him just the day before. You feel such a twit.

It was a shame I wasn't in love with him longer, because he was nice. He was very d. indeed and not a bit a rotter. I didn't actually tell him I wasn't in love with him; he just sort of gathered. I think really what it was, it was his trousers. I didn't look at his legs the first three days. He was quite amusing so there wasn't any need to. I mean if someone's talking away to you, you don't usually look at their legs. Then when I saw him the fourth day I suddenly noticed. His legs I mean. Well, not his actual legs, but his trousers. They were huge square things. Enormous square baggy billowy things. I couldn't love him any more after that. I wanted to but I just couldn't. For heaven's sake, they were like the things my father wears. My father's all right, but not even his best friend could say he had swoony legs.

What that man did do, though. He cured me of having a complex about my hips. I've got these huge hips. No really. Enormous. And he liked them. I mean, he said they weren't ugly a bit, and suddenly I didn't mind about them anymore. I did before. I used to keep my coat on for hours and hours because I thought everyone would die if they saw them. At parties I'd keep it on the whole evening in case no one would talk to me if they saw them. And I did anything to make people walk out of restaurants in front of me. No really. I'd say anything rather than have them walk behind me, and if they did I could feel their eyes boring into my back. And I thought they probably felt terribly sorry for me, and went on seeing me from pity. But that man he even went on liking them after he'd seen me in a swim-suit. 'Course he might have been blind with love, but I was too thrilled to think of that. It's marvellous when you stop minding about things. 'Specially about your hips. Anyway, they're such big things to mind about. Honestly, you should see them.

9

I think me being hours on the telephone to that man really got my father down. Anyway he decided that finally he had to get me off his mind. And earning money. So he wrote to this office he knows very well and said, did they want any more secretaries? And they said yes. So I filled in all those forms they make you fill in. You know. What sex? What sex are your parents? Are they sure? Are you a vampire? All that. Then this woman wrote and asked me to come for an interview. Only because she knew my father I think. Anyway I went.

Interviews are just as bad as you think they're going to be. First of all you don't know what to wear and then when you get there you can't remember whether you ate onions for lunch, so you spend the whole time mumbling sideways in case you did. Then you know you're going to hiccup so you have to cover it up with a coughing fit and they ask you if you've had a medical, and, if you haven't, look doubtful about whether you're TB. And, when they tell you about what sort of job it is, you know you're going to hate every minute of it. And they usually say they only take on nice girls. So you try and look madly nice and know you're going to loathe all the other nice girls. Sometimes I think I'd rather be a tart than go to another interview. Still, I suppose even if you're a tart you have to be interviewed by a pimp. So you're back where you started.

By the time they said yes they would have me, it was the last thing I wanted to do, be a secretary in that old office. I nearly died when they said they'd have me. Still, my father was pushing really hard, so I'd had it. Anyway there's always the chance you might get run over on your way there. Or have a heart attack on the bus.

The first morning I went there that's what I did. I sat on the bus praying I'd have a heart attack. I didn't have one though. I spent most of the morning filling in more forms and then they sent me off to have lunch with this girl. I didn't know what to say to her. We had this ham salad so I talked about ham for quite a lot of the time. I could see she wasn't interested in ham, but I couldn't think of anything else.

Then we stomped along to this room where all these secretaries worked. And she introduced me to them all, one by one. They all tried to look as if they weren't very interested, but I knew they were. Not nice interested either. I knew they were all hating me before I even said hello, because they knew who my father was. Honestly, you die inside when you know people are hating you, because nothing you say seems to sound all right. So you end up not saying anything. Just smiling vacantly at your typewriter.

This girl who was in charge started telling me very quietly in a corner what the work was about and what I had to do and everything. But I couldn't hear a word she was saying. The thing was she was saying all these things very quietly into my deaf ear. I've got this deaf ear, and when people say things very quietly into it I can't hear a thing. I didn't dare say I couldn't hear a thing she was saying. I thought she'd probably think I was being too grand to listen. So I sat the whole afternoon nodding and agreeing and not hearing a word. Honestly, it was really embarrassing. 'Specially the next morning when I couldn't understand a word of what I was doing.

The first week they didn't put me to work for anyone. They just gave me things to type and letters to copy. That was embarrassing too, because I could only type terribly slowly because I hadn't done a job for such ages. And I knew they were all watching to see how fast I was going. So after every two lines I'd look round and give this shaky laugh. You try it, honestly it's no joke. Typing and giving shaky laughs all day long. You just think you'll never be able to stop. You think you're going to be there sweating and typing for the rest of your life. No really. Your whole life.

One thing about this office. They had terribly long coffee and tea breaks. Not just a cup at your desk, you went to this room and sat at tables and everything. 'Course the first week I was there no one much spoke to me, so I went to coffee and tea every day with these same two girls. It was much worse than typing. Honestly, I used to sit there longing to be back sweating at my typewriter. The thing was I knew they were just dying to get me out of the way and say a few splendidly catty things about me and my typing. Only they couldn't because I was there and they were meant to be seeing I had someone to have coffee with.

You should have heard what they did talk about, these two girls. It was fantastic – day after day. They talked about how they washed their cardigans. And once they'd washed them they asked each other if they'd shrunk, and whether they should iron them. It wasn't that they couldn't talk about anything else, they just didn't want to. If I sort of murmured about something else they carried on talking about these old cardigans as if I wasn't there. Once I asked one of them if she had a boyfriend, and she looked so offended you'd think I'd asked her something much worse. It Though actually it's often the po-type girl that's mad about sex. They sit about looking very respectable and the next minute they're buying a smock.

'Course it's the old, old story when you get bags of women all working on top of each other. They just sit about knitting and talking about each other. If they haven't much imagination that's all they can think of doing. And once they've been doing it for a long time they couldn't stop if they wanted. Also they get this thing, like people in prison. They mind passionately about the tiniest things. Even things like whose turn to shut the window. And quarrel like anything for hours before they decide. It really matters to them whose turn it is. I don't think it does in the beginning, but I suppose after a bit they just get like everyone else. And they are in a prison. Only not the kind you can get out of.

None of these women liked me. I didn't really blame them. I don't think I'd have liked me if I'd been them either. It was awful at first because it was so lonely. When you've been a failure you mind about people not liking you. It really worries you. Because you're just a different kind of failure. But still a failure. Do you know I used to sit having coffee with those women, and sometimes I really wondered if we were all speaking English. No really. I could have been speaking Eskimo for all they knew or cared. And the awful thing was there were so many of them, and only one of me. You can scream with laughter if you've got someone else, but it's practically impossible to laugh by yourself. Every now and then I did though. Very privately behind my typewriter. But it was hardly living it up. I mean I can think of things I've done that were gayer.

Still, you can only mind about things up to a point. Once you've really done your nut about them, they cease to matter anymore. Even being lonely you get like that. You mind like anything, then suddenly it just seems splendidly funny and you'd rather die than not be alone among a lot of tiny-minded women. I got more and more eccentric when I was in that office. I had to prove the whole day long that I wasn't like them. Honestly, I'd have gone about naked to prove to myself I wasn't. Because every now and then I used to have awful nightmares that I was like them. Or I was becoming like them. Or I would become like them any minute. I'd wake up and find myself knitting and talking about Miss Smith's green hair. Gradually it would creep up on me. I wouldn't know it was happening but one day I'd wake up and I'd be a petty old thing sniping away making some poor little spotty secretary's life a misery. That's a feminine art that some women have to perfection. It's funny, it's nothing you can put your hand on. They don't swear and scream at you, but very quietly they make you depressed. And yet you couldn't say what it was. You really couldn't. It's like that tap-dripping torture. I mean, what's an old tap dripping anyway?

Though it was all right for me. I had a cushy time of it compared to some people. I had weeds and parties and jokey parents and no spots. But imagine what it's like if you're weedless and parentless and you go home to your bed-sitter in the evening, only to eat, sleep, and then take the Tube again to face tiny minds for another eight hours. And on top of that you've got some old bitch sniping away at you. And you can't get another job, because you're afraid. I could have left any day, I only didn't because I wanted to prove I could stay in a job. I mean you feel sorry for those bitches till you see them torturing little asthmatic secretaries with runny noses. Hell, I was fair game.

I nearly went to live with an awful smooth man from working in that office. Honestly, I was mad. I mean if you've got to live with someone it really shouldn't be some awful smooth slug. It was all part of proving madly that I wasn't becoming a net-curtain semi-detached typist. I wanted to be a bosomy sex symbol. One of those women from movie posters: 'Men loved and hated her. She was fire to the blood. No man had been known to forget her.'

I don't know why I even felt tempted to live with the slug. Except he wanted me to. But mostly when people ask me I shriek with laughter. I didn't with him. He was the first weed who even tempted me. And yet I didn't love him in the least. I suppose I was flattered at being fire to someone's blood. Even a smooth slug. And he couldn't have been smoother. Honestly, everything about him. He was good-looking, but in a very smooth way. He was smoothly intelligent, smoothly amusing, smoothly attentive. He had a smooth car and a smooth flat and he smoked smooth cigarettes.

Also he was smoothly seductive. He made you feel very silly because you wouldn't sleep with him. Not furious or anything. Just very silly. Actually it's funny about when men are trying to seduce you. You think up every reason. Like you're religious, your mother wouldn't like it, you respect them too much, all the corniest things. And the one thing you never think of is, you'd rather die than sleep with them and they make you feel quite sick anyway.

But this smooth man didn't make me feel sick. That was the trouble. It would have been easy if he'd made me feel sick. Not only didn't he make me feel sick, he made me laugh. When people make you feel a little foolish and make you laugh too it seems stupid. Particularly sometimes when you feel sad about not finding another superman. It was Migo who stopped me turning into a smooth mistress of a smooth slug. She said, imagine if I got smoothly pregnant and had to get smoothly married and live smoothly ever after in that smooth flat. I couldn't take that. I really couldn't. Imagine having a smooth breakfast every morning. And watching him eat smooth boiled eggs. It would kill me.

Then Chloë came to work in this office. She was at school with Migo and me. She was going to be an actress, but she couldn't stand everyone stabbing everyone in the back. Anyway that's what she said.

So she got down to being an old secretary like me. It made it much better, Chloë being there actually, because she was pretty jokey. She couldn't do shorthand to save her life, and I don't think she knew how to wash a cardigan either. We both worked for two people in the same room, and we'd have secret signs to each other when we were taking dictation. Endless sunny afternoons we'd sit pretending we were in bikinis gambolling on beaches with bronzed men. That's one thing; if you've got imagination, they can never really stop you dreaming. It takes a bit of imagination to pretend you're on a beach when you're doing shorthand.

It really wasn't bad being in that office with Chloë. Once you've got one other person to laugh with you're all right. That's the worst thing, whatever you're doing, not having someone to laugh with. I should think hell would be all right if you had some other sinner to joke with. You could spend the whole time screaming with laughter at the devil. I bet he's an awful ham anyway.

Chloë went on being very jokey till she fell in love. She fell in love with this frightfully rich man. I felt sorry for her, because it's practically impossible to be jokey when you're in love. Admittedly she wanted to be in love. Most girls do. They don't feel all right unless they're in love or having a broken heart. Chloë never really wasn't in love or broken-hearted when I knew her. When she first started working in that office with me she was broken-hearted. She was being gay and jokey to cover up that her life was ruined. Then once she'd fallen in love again she was happy. She'd got something to suffer about. She used to stay at the office being overworked when he wasn't taking her out. She sat looking noble and carrying bravely on with shorthand in spite of everything, ages after we'd all gone home. And she used to lean against the filing-cupboards and sigh. She always looked as if she had drapey things on. She didn't actually. Only scarves and things tied round her which she spent the whole time looping about. 'Specially on her extra droopy days.

She lived in this flat in Fulham with three other girls. I went and had supper with them once or twice. They were a pretty funny lot. In fact the whole place was pretty funny. It had a funny atmosphere. It hit you when you walked in the door. Not only me. It hit Migo too. She noticed it as well as me. It wasn't Chloë really, it was these other three girls. They prowled about all looking the same. They had this funny look in their eyes. Very nervous and as if they were waiting all the time for something. No really they did.

Migo and I called them the waiting women. 'Course basically they were all just looking around for supermen, I suppose. Only more than most girls. They just didn't think about anything else. Not one other thing. They were just waiting around for the telephone, or the door, or the post. They never actually did anything except wait around. I suppose that's why they had this funny look in their eyes. Chloë was the only one that did anything like a job. I think it made her a bit po being among all those waiting women. She wasn't po naturally. Stagey but not po.

Two of those waiting women were frightfully morbid and nervy. The post was always not going to come, the telephone was never going to ring. It really got me down all the bells that weren't going to ring. And the other one was frightfully smarty-smarty. One has one's hair done at the Queen's hairdresser, one's writing paper comes from the Queen's stationer, one's weekends in Berks, Bucks, or Wilts, and one meets one's girlfriends for lunch once a week at Harrods. And one swoons over teeny-minded weeds in Knightsbridge flats.

One of those morbid girls told me about this man she was in love with. She was in love with him, for heaven's sake. She actually told me she loved him, and then she said the most disgusting thing I've ever heard about him. Honestly, I felt sorry for the man having her in love with him, even if it was true. When I told Chloë she just laughed and said if I knew the man I'd say the same thing. She couldn't understand that it's pretty warped to say things like that about someone you're meant to be in love with. She was funny like that, Chloë. She really was.

She used to tell me about this frightfully rich man. She said being in love with him was like diving into a deep pool. That's what she said. I couldn't understand her. I said I thought I'd been in love but I didn't think it was like diving into a deep pool. She said I wasn't mature. She said if I was mature I'd understand. Only mature people understood. She could be pretty boring like that. She used to get frightfully cross with Migo and I when we made jokes. 'Specially jokes about love. She said making jokes about love was immature.

I went out to lunch with these girls and Chloë every now and then. They all sat in this coffee bar and talked about clothes and hair. That was all right. Then they'd start talking about other girls' clothes and hair.

That was really boring. You should have heard them. No one was all right. They always spoiled themselves. Honestly, I never heard them talk about someone who was all right all over. They always spoiled themselves with too much make-up or too short skirts, or they were too tarty or too dull. And if they were fat they should go on a diet, and if they were thin then of course men hated girls who were thin like that. And you wouldn't know the poor wretch was a girl at all, if you saw her from behind, you'd think she was a boy. She was just a clothes-peg. And they'd all rather die than be like that. Men liked women to be women.

There was one other thing they talked about. That was who was engaged or married or pregnant. That was pretty funny too. If the man wasn't a drip, then she was getting married because she had to, and everyone knew why she had an Empire-line wedding dress. They'd sit for hours counting up how many months between when she got married and had the baby. And of course it could have been a seven months' baby. But it was pretty funny because they were usually small and someone had seen it and it was huge. That kind of conversation is pretty sad.

Anyhow they decided to share a party with Migo and I and hold it in their flat. We sent millions of invitations to weeds and drips all over London. And they all came. The waiting women were thrilled. It was the only thing they lived for, just to have millions of weeds to swoon over. It was going to be a weed feast.

It was the usual sort of bodies-everywhere party that people give in Fulham. Bodies among coats, furniture, glasses, behind the dustbin, in the bath – everywhere. Routine types. I fell asleep in a cupboard half-way through because someone put something in my drink. I didn't really care because it saved me the boredom of introducing more weeds to more drippy girls. Some girls are so drippy at parties it's embarrassing. They either make straight for the food and stand stuffing their faces or sit about telling other girls how awful they think all the weeds are. Or they come looking beautiful and expect everyone to swoon up and talk to them because they're beautiful. By the end you could strangle them. I don't know why they come sometimes. Honestly I don't.

When I crawled out of that cupboard the party was practically over. It was pretty funny actually. I mean it's not every day you wake up and find yourself surrounded by dresses and hangers. Then I couldn't get the door open because some couple were having a passionate scene against it. They looked a bit surprised to see me crawl out. Then they just went on having their passionate scene. They weren't the only ones. All over the floor these couples were having great scenes, and in the middle of them sitting up in bed with a nightie on was old Chloë. She had face-cream on and was putting curlers in her hair. It didn't worry her all these scenes going on. She's good like that. She was going to bed, and that was it. She's very particular about her sleep actually. It really worries her if she doesn't get her right amount. It makes her skin sag. Anyway that's what she says.

I went into the kitchen and found a little spotty man trying to light the oven. Well, turn the gas on anyway. I said, why did he want to turn the oven on? And he said he wanted to put his head in it. I said couldn't he find something else to do, putting your head in the oven isn't a swoony way to spend a party. Even a bad party. He said, no, he had to put his head in the oven, he'd promised someone faithfully that he would. He'd given his word he would. He never went back on his word. Never. I said I hated to make him break his word, but the oven didn't work. So he burst into tears all over the kitchen table, and I gave him a dish-cloth to wipe his tears. Poor little spotty man. I forgot to ask him why he had to put his head in the oven.

Chloë never saw her rich man after that party. So she went back to being bravely happy again. I preferred her being bravely happy to being in love. And the waiting women went back to waiting, and listening for their bells. Nutcase lot. And the awful thing is they'll be worse when they're married. Because when you wait around for something and never think about anything else you're always disappointed. And disappointed married women are hell. They spend the whole time being just thirty, and having shoulder-length hair and reading historical novels. No, it's true. Really. I know lots of women like that. They're the end, they really are.

I've always been mad on the theatre. I suppose it's pretty corny. My mother writes plays so it's not surprising really. She's been writing plays ever since I can remember. I used to go and eat kippers with my grandmother because she had to go to rehearsals. When I fell in love with that actor she used to blame herself for it. She said I wouldn't have fallen in love with him if she hadn't written plays.

I don't know a lot of actors. A few but not a lot. Mostly I think they're more amusing than ordinary people. A lot of people still talk about them as if they weren't being buried in holy ground for heaven's sake. Especially my grandmother. She calls them 'theatricals'. Anything she says about them she always says at the end, 'What can you expect of theatricals?' When I used to eat kippers with her she always said, 'I hope your mother doesn't bring any of those theatricals back with her.' And when I said, 'Why?' she said they had filthy habits.

My mother had a play on when I was at school. It was pretty exciting for me. And for the nuns too. They spent the whole time praying it would be a success, but it wasn't. It was very disappointing after all those prayers. What I said to one nun was, perhaps God didn't like the play. You don't know, do you? It just might not have been the kind of thing that made Him laugh. Not His sort of play.

During my holidays my mother often used to take me to see actors and people to try and get them interested in her plays. Mostly they weren't very swoony about them. One or two of them were, but not many. My mother said you couldn't blame them. She said they only really had time to be interested in who was going to put them into plays. She said being an actor wasn't funny. It was sad, really. Because of being out of work, and staying at home waiting for an agent to ring. Also hoping you could pay the phone bill.

My father doesn't swoon about actors. That one I was in love with was the only one he really liked. He looks a bit strange when they call him darling. And he tries to swoon when they tell him about when Bobby lost his wig and Geoffrey had to walk on with the book under the bedpan. But he can't. It's not really *him*. I don't think he'd go to the theatre much if it wasn't for my mother. Anyway he says he hates the intervals. That's why he likes the movies better because there aren't any intervals. He says it's like someone telling you a story and then going off to the loo in the middle.

He has one thing just like me, my father. If he goes to a movie he always comes out *being* whoever he's seen. My mother doesn't. She doesn't understand a bit, she's just going on being herself when she comes out. But my father, if he's seen Hannibal, he's being Hannibal for at least two hours afterwards. Or if he's seen a war movie he's being frightfully stiff upper lip, and I'm the same. If I see some huge sex symbol I'm a huge sex symbol, and if I see some playful sprite then I'm being a playful sprite. It's pretty annoying when my mother goes on being herself though. I mean, if you're being Hannibal, you don't want to be asked to go and get someone's slippers.

Then someone bought another of my mother's plays. And I used to stomp off to rehearsals with her. Watching rehearsals I decided I didn't think I'd like to be an actress after all. I used to think it would be marvellous. I still think it's all right but not marvellous. Everyone's so nervy and smoky at rehearsals. I don't think I'd have the guts to act away with everyone being nervy and smoky round me. For heaven's sake, I can't even type with people being nervy and smoky. No, honestly, I can't. My fingers go all stiff.

Also people seem rather shouty at rehearsals. They don't just say rude words to each other – they shout them. I can't bear people shouting at me. I don't mind if they talk in a loud voice, but if they shout right at me my eyes go all watery and I can't do anything. I get like that even when I'm on a horse. No, it's true. If someone shouts at me when I'm on a horse my eyes go all watery and I nearly fall off.

One of the actresses in my mother's play had a daughter about my age. We often got left together and we used to have little chats, mostly about the theatre. She was very pretty. More than pretty actually, and more than beautiful. And very nice. Nervous but very nice. She was the only person who was sympathetic when the play was a flop. Not just because her mother was in it either. It's always pretty dull when a play is a flop. Everyone blames everyone else. But she was sympathetic without being corny. Lots of people when they're being sympathetic just make you want to nun off.

I didn't see her again for ages and ages, then she suddenly rang me up and came to see me. She was madly in love with a fascinating man, and she chatted away about it. Then she said she was pregnant I found myself thinking that I hadn't heard quite right – on account of my bad ear and all that. I knew I mustn't look sorry for her, although I did. I settled for looking dumb, which I am quite good at now. Actually, I really did feel sorry for her. I had the feeling that she didn't quite know what had happened to her. It was as if she didn't know how babies were born. She was a bit like me on Bognor Beach that time. She couldn't believe what someone had told her. I mean, babies always seem to be something that happen to other people.

Anyway, we sort of left it at that. Probably because I didn't know what to say, and she married the fascinating man, and six months later she had the baby. I met them in the park one day and she still looked as if she didn't quite know what had happened to her, how she came to be pushing a pram. It was as if she had borrowed the pram, and the baby.

My mother blamed her mother for not telling her about affairs leading to babies. My grandmother didn't blame anyone, she just cleared her throat very loudly, because she doesn't approve of people having babies at all.

I'm not sure that my mother wasn't right. I mean you have to know about affairs leading to babies and prams, even if, like me, you don't quite like being told about how it all happens on Bognor Beach.

That girl was the first time I realised that people got themselves into things rather than live happily ever after. No honestly. Of course I knew that some people didn't. But they weren't really people I knew very well. I just always took it for granted that you live happily ever after. My parents have lived happily ever after by and large. They really have. I think my father gets a bit browned off with getting hot-water bottles for headaches sometimes, and my mother wouldn't mind him being a bit richer, but on the whole they've lived happily ever after.

Not many girls' parents live happily ever after. I only know about two girls' parents who have. Even if they're not divorced or something, they've usually got lovers. Lovers are corny. They're so normal. Someone's going to have to invent something else. No honestly.

That's the trouble now really. You just can't find anything to do that's going to shock anyone. Honestly, it's pretty miserable not being able to shock anyone. There's nothing you can do that people won't yawn at if you tell them about it. You can't even surprise them by being naked. A friend of mine went to a party naked.

Nothing on at all. She had her coat on to arrive in but nothing underneath. You'd think people would be a bit surprised but they weren't at all. She said they hardly noticed at all. Mind you, it was quite dark. Even so, you'd think they'd be a bit taken back. She said one person said what a nice pink dress she had on but that's all.

One thing though. I wish fat women were admired now. I do honestly. I wish huge great fleshy women were what men swooned over. I'm not exactly a huge fat woman on the beach. But jolly near. Mostly it's my hips actually. I've got one friend, it's her back. She's thin all over except for this back. I don't think fleshy women will come back. They're just not practical I suppose. What with buses and things. You couldn't get them all on.

Slimming's one of my hobbies really. Migo and I. I should think we've done every diet you can do. Migo's as thin as anything. She just does them to keep me company. In case I get discouraged. It's not that I like eating. I just like a little something every now and then. And that's why I've got hips. I went to this doctor once and he said my hips were just due to little somethings. Some people smoke and I have little somethings. I've tried to smoke but I'm no good.

That's my ambition. To be smoky and thin. I don't know if I ever will be. On the whole I think you've got to be more nervy than me. Perhaps I'll be more nervy when I'm older. A lot of people are.

Not many of my relations are hippy like me. Plump all over but not hippy. I've got an awful lot of relations. None of them is what you'd do your nut over. Mostly they're cousins. They don't really care about me and I don't think I really care about them. They'd just be useful if you were an orphan. They're not even real cousins. Most of them are removed in some way. And they come stomping up to you at parties and go on about you being one of their cousins. I bet if you were a lavatory attendant they'd soon forget you were. I shouldn't think they'd even know you. Let alone go about telling everyone you were their cousin.

My mother's hobbies are slimming and dailies. She swears every evening after a huge dinner that she'll go on a diet. Cut down on sherry and everything. She's still on it at breakfast the next morning but by lunch she just feels it's her duty to eat up all the left-overs. She says someone's got to. And if she doesn't no one will. She can't bear to see waste. She says it's because of the war. That's what ruined her figure – not being able to bear waste during the war.

Anyhow her other hobby is dailies. She says dailies are more interesting than most people. She has these long conversations with them. About practically everything. She says there's practically nothing a daily doesn't know. One thing she doesn't like much. She doesn't like their operations. She's not much good on operations. Some people are mad on them. They talk about them for hours and hours. And they know all the names of what these operations are called. I don't mind the names, it's when they're actually describing them I don't like it. Once a woman told me about having a bit of her body removed. It was terrible. I felt for the rest of the day I had to keep looking down to see I hadn't got a gap. It's terrible when you feel all gappy. Anyhow, that's where my mother gets all the plots for her plays. From all these dailies she talks to.

I'm not keen on operations but I like medicines and pills and glucose. I think it's working in an office that's made me like that. I'm so bored I feel every twinge. So I take all these things to get me through the day. Honestly, it makes the day go much quicker if you take pills and glucose. Also they make something to look at. It's pretty boring just looking at your typewriter or the wall or someone's face. I get this feeling I've got no energy because I yawn so much. I had a boyfriend, he was the same. He was a lawyer so he took glucose and pills in between clients. We used to go round chemists together and find new things to take. And he'd ring me up and remind me when to take them. We thought of founding a club for bored glucose-eaters, but he got sent to Manchester so it was no good.

Migo was having quite a boring time too. She was a secretary only she couldn't do shorthand at all. She was the only person I'd ever met who was worse than me. Only her job wasn't as boring as mine, it really wasn't. But she was in love with a footballer, which was pretty awful. Footballers are awful people to be in love with. First of all they never ever love anyone better than their footballs. My cousin told me. She was in love with one too. Then every Saturday they go stomping off and you have to watch them for hours and hours as they kick this football around, then afterwards they drink beer and talk to all these other men who have been kicking it around too. They hardly ever speak to you except during the week. And then they're very tired from having kicked this football around on Saturdays. I don't know what their fascination is really. My cousin says it's probably these shorts they wear on Saturdays. Also they're very muscly. I don't like muscly men, but she does, and she says when they're in these shorts you can see their muscles.

Migo said it was probably their muscles in these shorts too. She didn't really know for sure, but she thought it probably was. Anyway, she used to listen to these very old records wearing his football scarf, and cry about him. It worried me seeing her listening to these records and crying about this footballer. But she said she enjoyed it. She said it did her good to listen to these records; they were really old actually. I mean they were so old you could hardly hear them. In fact, if I had my deaf ear near the gramophone I couldn't hear them at all.

It took her a long time to get over the footballer. I made her burn his scarf and buy jazz records, but it still wasn't too swoony for her. There really ought to be a purge you could take to get over being in love. Even when you burn a scarf it still doesn't stop you feeling gone inside. It didn't stop Migo. She felt all gone inside every time she even saw a football for heaven's sake.

When she'd got over the footballer, she met her superman. He really is a superman actually. Even my mother thinks he's a superman and it takes quite a lot for her to think that. No really. She only just thinks my father is a superman. Of course she does think he is, but only just.

Chloë and I were bridesmaids when Migo got married. Chloë was very sad because Migo is younger than her. She hates anyone younger than her getting married. She says it makes her feel unsuccessful. Actually I think Chloë goes in for being sad because she knows it suits her. She has these very large brown eyes and when she looks sad they look marvellous. Now Migo's married Chloë's learning to appreciate beautiful things. No, it's true, practically every Saturday she goes about appreciating beautiful things. She says that destiny has not mapped out a married life for her. Not for her a superman. And she says it's just not in her nature to marry anyone but a superman. She can't help being a perfectionist. So she's appreciating beautiful things before her eyesight goes. I don't know though. If Migo found a superman I don't see why old Chloë shouldn't. Or anyone else for that matter.

1 1

My grandmother says it's unnatural sitting here scribbling. She says I should be out looking for a rich superman instead of being cooped up. I probably am unnatural actually. I mean, what's the point of sitting here talking about all these weeds and drips and things and not doing something about finding a superman? It's just I thought you might like to know. I've probably been as boring as hell. But I just thought I'd have a go at telling you.

Actually you've probably gathered by now a superman takes some finding. They're not things you just come across like that. One friend of mine, she's been looking for one since God was a boy. No luck. Weeds and drips. No superman. She asked me if I thought there was any special place where she might find one. I don't think there is. I don't know, mind you. But I don't think so. I've never been there anyway.

One thing though. I think you can class most men. Superman, weed, drip, lech. I only met one person you couldn't. He wasn't a superman. He wasn't a weed or a drip. And he wasn't a lech. He was a womaniser but he wasn't a lech. He was only a womaniser when he felt all gone inside. He felt it quite a lot really. What he was, I think, was a vagabond. He was the only person I've ever met who was. A lot of people wander about. But not many are real vagabonds. He was a real vagabond.

I once tried to get two friends of mine to come and be vagabonds with me. But it was no use. They were just no good. All they did was wonder what would they do about money? And they couldn't leave their parents. They just had no idea how to begin to be vagabonds. When I was ten I wrote a poem about wanting to be a vagabond. And I ran away from my school to be one. It was a pretty good idea. Only these three other girls I was with didn't want to do anything but go home. It's pretty frustrating, I can tell you, when you're running away to be a vagabond and you've got all these people just wanting to go home. And it's no good being a vagabond on your own. You must have someone to be poetic with too.

My mother was furious when I ran away from school. She couldn't understand about being a vagabond. She just said if I did it again she'd take me away and send me to a really horrible school. She said it was ungrateful when she'd taken all the trouble to send me to a nice school and all I did was run away. What she was really furious about was this policeman's wife who gave us a huge tea when we got fed up with running away. She couldn't get over us having three boiled eggs each. I said we hadn't had anything to eat all day. And she said I wasn't to answer back. That's what they spend the whole time saying to you when you're young. They ask you something, then when you tell them they say you're answering back and you've given quite enough trouble to everyone without answering back.

When we did get back to school they shut us in our rooms for three days. And this matron walked us in the gardens when all the school was having lunch. They didn't want us spreading evil all over the other girls. She carried a rosary in one hand this matron, when she was walking us. She said it was protection from the devils in us. She was Irish. And she told us that we'd all burn in hell, and she was praying to save our souls from damnation. She said she didn't think it would do much good but anyway she was having a go. She said she wasn't one to give up hope, not till the very end.

It was pretty boring sitting in our rooms for three days. But we used to tap on the walls to each other and pass bubble-gum on our toothbrushes through the windows. And one or two of the other girls' parents came down to see them in the parlour. Mine didn't thank goodness. They just wrote me these terribly long, cross letters. Still, it was better than having them in the parlour any day.

If I actually told you how I met this real vagabond, you wouldn't believe me. No honestly, you'd just think I was a loon. I met him walking along a road. No, it's true. I was staying with these people in the country. I quite like staying with people in the country. But I get a bit bored after a bit. So often I go for walks by myself and sing and bash hedges with a stick. Because most people you stay with think you're a bit funny if you sing and bash hedges with sticks when they're around.

I was bashing away walking along this road and singing to myself. I can't sing. Well, it's not exactly that I can't sing. Apparently I've got a voice but I just can't sing in tune. When I bumped into this man in front of me. He was just walking along with his hands in his pockets. I just went on singing and bashing away, when he turned off down this drive. It was a very long straight drive with stone gates. You know the kind. And waving trees and deer in the park bit on each side. The kind of drive you die to get on a horse and zoom up with important news.

I stopped when he went down this drive and watched him walking down. It was a very sunny day. Sunny and breezy and he walked in a whistley sort of way. Corny, but you know what I mean. And I felt awfully jealous watching him. I don't know why. I just stood by these stone gates and wished I was walking down this drive in a whistley sort of way too. He was just getting to the top and practically out of sight when I gave a yell. I don't know why I gave that yell either. Actually most marvellous things that you do, you don't know why you do them till you have.

He stopped, when I gave this yell, and turned round. And I ran like anything all the way up this drive. When I reached him he didn't seem surprised to see me at all. That's the best bit about vagabonds, they're never surprised. No, honestly. Real vagabonds wouldn't be surprised if you came out of a hole in the ground. I panted a bit when I reached him and he just stood smiling at me. Then I said, did he live there? And he said yes. So I said I wanted to see round. So he said, okay he'd show me. Just like that.

Don't you think that about all really marvellous things? They're *so* corny. When you tell anyone about them afterwards anyhow. I bet Napoleon felt corny when he was telling everyone about retreating from Moscow. Come to think of it, I don't suppose that was marvellous. But you know what I mean. Perhaps that's why they're marvellous. Because they're corny-corny. And magical and enchanting. That's what that day I spent with the vagabond was like. I spent this whole day wandering round his house with him and walking in his garden. He rang up the people I was staying with and said he was an old friend and could I have lunch with him? For heaven's sake it was like something in a movie.

And his house was like a movie. Beautiful tall rooms and long windows. So you could just step through them and be in the garden. We had lunch in the garden and it was the most beautiful garden you've ever been in. No really. It was all fountains and lawns and shady trees. Like some people think Heaven will be like. It won't half be bad if it is, I can tell you.

I wish I could describe this vagabond without making him sound corny. I can't remember his face. Not all his features anyway. Except he had blue eyes and very white teeth. Though perhaps they only looked white because he had this very brown skin. And he was thin and had a very deep voice. And he was sad. Well, it wasn't that he was droopy or anything. Because he laughed a lot. He just had this terribly sad quality about him. Like a very happy song that catches in your throat.

And he was easy to talk to. Honestly, I don't remember word for word what we talked about. But we never stopped. It was just non-stop. If anyone else had been there they'd have been bored stiff. No honestly, they would. I told him things I usually just think and don't tell anyone about. Things most people look really embarrassed if you tell them about them. As if you'd forgotten to put your clothes on or something.

He told me about this woman he'd loved. He really had loved her. No really. And he knew what an awful thing love was. I said I'd never known anything more awful and he agreed. What happened with this woman he loved was they loved too much. He said they loved so much they destroyed each other. He said that was why he was a womaniser now. And also he got drunk. He knew what all gone inside meant all right, he really did.

I suppose that's why he had this sad feeling about him. Because of having loved so much. I told him about only having been in love once. With this actor. I said most people just said it was infatuation. But he said it sounded like love all right. He said from what I'd told him it didn't sound like infatuation. What he said too was not to get depressed about it. He said it was much worse never to have known what love was really like than to have loved someone and gone away and been unhappy about it. He said some people never knew what it was like. He said they never would know. Not necessarily just narrow little people either. Often imaginative people who were quite super didn't know what it was like. It just wasn't in them to love like that.

He really could talk, this vagabond. And he could tell you about anything. Like someone people in books are always meeting. Only I'd never met someone like that before. I never have since, come to think of it. He's the only one. All the things you believe in your heart but you're not quite sure you're not a nit believing in them. He made you sure. When he told you about things. Suddenly you knew you were right to believe in them. You knew they weren't corny like most people thought they were. It was only the people that thought them corny that were.

He made you so certain you were right you could burst. You just thought you must have been mad before not to have been sure. And you were never going to not be sure again. Like when you're happy. You're never going to not be happy again. And you can't remember what you were unhappy about before.

He made you not mind about being *you*. Not being someone who cared about corny old abortions. Not mind about having big hips or a pretty funny face. Or anything. Nothing mattered because here was someone who believed, who believed in magic and enchantment. And everything when he was talking was magic and enchantment. Even me. I suddenly knew I was fascinating and magical too. It's pretty marvellous when you sit in an office all day with people minding about whose turn it is to shut the window when you meet someone who believes in magic. And makes you feel fascinating. Not a plump secretary who can't do shorthand. It's okay to be a plump secretary who can't do shorthand. But it's awful when you *feel* a plump secretary who can't do shorthand.

I never went back to see that vagabond. I've never stayed with those people again either. So he might be dead now for all I know. Or just womanising round the place. Or perhaps he's making someone else feel fascinating. Perhaps his house has been sold to someone who won't ever want to step through the window into the garden. I don't know.

I just know I won't ever go back. You can never make a bigger mistake than going back. The only reason to go back is to try and recapture. And how can you recapture magic? You don't even know what it is for heaven's sake. And how can you get back something when you don't even know what it is? I don't know what it is. I just know I believe in it. And I didn't know what the vagabond's name was. I forgot to ask him. He asked me mine. But I forgot to ask him. It wasn't important anyway.

I don't only believe in magic. I believe in everything corny. I believe that there is a superman. Somewhere. I believe in love. My mother says I'll end up staring in a two-roomed flat in Hampstead because I do. She says it's the worst thing to believe in. I don't care. I do. And I believe in innocence. You can't stop me. I'm always going to believe in it. Yes I am. Even if I don't find a superman.

I don't think anyone's a failure as long as they're still innocent. Just a little. They may lose everything good in them but as long as they believe just a little in something very small, they're still innocent. To fail is to lose every bit of innocence.

And innocence needn't be beautiful. That's the trouble when you're young – you think there's nothing innocent unless it's beautiful. There are all these millions of things that hurt you because they're not beautiful. No honestly, you go round being practically killed by all these things that are ugly – then when you're nearly killed, you suddenly laugh. Once you laugh you're all right. If you think, jolly few things laugh. I've got a friend who swears his cat laughs. But it's not what you'd notice. You can't actually hear it when it laughs. And once I was on a bus and there was this big fat woman roaring with laughter. She didn't stop from the time she got on. And do you know, all those people on that bus – me too – started laughing. All these frightfully dull business men and po old housewives and everything. They all began to roar with laughter. Just because of this woman laughing. And they all looked quite different. They stopped looking constipated and po and looked happy. Mostly, though, I should think humans are the only things that laugh. Laughing is what makes humans human.

A lot of people just run away instead though. They don't give themselves time to stop and find something to make them laugh. They run away and start sneering because it's hurting them. Or they run away and just find a swoony spot to hide in so they don't have to see things that hurt. If they really went on looking at something that hurt them they'd realise it was beautiful, and it would probably make them scream with laughter too. Mind you, you've got to stick at it.

I'll tell you another corny thing. I'd like to write a love poem to the world. Really I would. Sometimes I love it so much.

It's always thinking it's the first to do things. The whole time it's doing things it keeps thinking no one's done it before. It thinks each war is the worst. Each civilisation the most civilised. Every king the most important. Every poet the most poetic. Each new joke the funniest – because it's so innocent. It keeps forgetting everything's happened before. And when we all go, the next version of the world will think it's the most important bit. And no one will think much about us having thought it all before them. Honestly, you tell me what's more innocent than the world? It's so innocent you can't help loving it.

ACKNOWLEDGEMENTS

My grateful thanks to Alexandra Pringle who remembered this book with such affection.

To Allegra Le Fanu and Angelique Tran Van Sang for putting up with my foibles and doing such a great editing job.

Last, but not least, to my agent Matthew Brady for his patience and encouragement, and my daughter Candida Brady-Ogilvy for her constant enthusiasm and support.

A NOTE ON THE AUTHOR

Charlotte Bingham wrote her first book, *Coronet Among the Weeds*, a memoir of her life as a debutante, at the age of 19. It was published in 1963 and became an instant bestseller. Her father, John Bingham, the 7th Baron Clanmorris, was a member of MI15 where Charlotte Bingham worked as a secretary. He was an inspiration for John le Carré's character George Smiley.

Charlotte Bingham went on to write thirty-three internationally bestselling novels and the memoir *MI5 and Me*. In partnership with her late husband Terence Brady, she wrote a number of successful plays, films and TV series including *Upstairs Downstairs* and *Take Three Girls*. She lives in Somerset.

charlottebingham.com